AA

EXPLORE BRITAIN'S
◆
COASTLINE

Produced by AA Publishing

EXPLORE BRITAIN'S
COASTLINE

by Richard Cavendish

AA Publishing, a trading name of Automobile Association Developments Limited, whose registered office is Norfolk House, Priestley Road, Basingstoke, Hampshire RG24 9NY. Registered number 1878835.

A catalogue record for this book is available from the British Library.

ISBN h/b 0 749 50681 4
          s/b 0 749 50771 3

Colour origination by L.C. Repro and Sons Ltd, Aldermaston.
Printed and bound by Graficromo SA, Cordoba, Spain.

The contents of this book are believed correct at the time of printing. Nevertheless, the Publishers cannot accept responsibility for errors or omissions, or for changes in details given.

Acknowledgements: all photographs and illustrations are held in the Automobile Association's own library with contributions as follows:

F/Cover J.Beazley, B/Cover S. Gregory, Spine R. Moss, 6/7 N.Ray, 10 H.Williams, 12, 13 A.Lawson, 14 T.Teegan, 15, 16 S&O Matthews, 18, 19 A.Lawson, 20 A.Hopkins, 21 A.Hopkins, 22 V & S.Bates, 23 R.Czaja, 24,25 N.Ray, 26/7 V.Sinhal, 29, 30 A.Lawson, 31a H.Williams, 31b S&O Matthews, 32 H.Williams, 33 W.Voysey, 34, 35 P.Baker, 36 W.Voysey, 38/9, 39 R.Fletcher, 41 S&O Matthews, 42/3 D.Forss, 44/5 P.Baker, 45 M.Trelawny, 46, 47 D.Forss, 48 P.Davies, 49 D.Forss, 50 S&O Matthews, 51 W.Voysey, 52/3 P.Baker, 53 D.Noble, 54 D.Corrance, 55 P.Baker, 56/7, 57, 58 D.Noble, 59 S&O Matthews, 60/1, 61 M.Birkitt, 62 P.Davies, 64 M.Birkitt, 65, 66/7, 68 S&O Matthews, 69 H.Williams, 70, 70/1, 71 P.Davies, 72 A.Perkins, 74, 75 S&O Matthews, 76 A.Hopkins, 78 A.Souter, 79 S&O Matthews, 79 A.Souter, 80/1 Goose (H.Burn), Fulmar (R.Gillmor), Guillemot (T.Boyer), Avocet/Oystercatcher (H.Burn), Shelduck (H.Burn), Eider (T.Boyer), Gull (C.Rose), 82 R.Surman, 83 P.Baker, 85 M.Adelman, 86 S.Gregory, 88/9 G.Rowatt, 90 R.Newton, 91 C.Molyneux, 92, 93, 94 S.Gregory, 96, 97, 98/9 J.Beazley, 100 S.King, 101 P.Sharp, 102 A.Lawson, 103 W.Voysey, 104, 105a, b M.Trelawny, 106/7 S.Bates, 107 S.Bates, 108/9 V.Greaves, 110 I.Burgum, 112 S&O Matthews, 113 R.Surman, 114 R.Newton, 115 D.Corrance, 116 D.Croucher, 118 R.Eames, 119 R.Newton, 120, 121 T.Timms, 122 H.Williams, 123 I.Burgum, 124 H.Williams, 126, 127, 128, 129, I.Burgum, 131 D.Noble, 132 M.Allwood-Coppin, 133 C.Molyneux, 134, 135 I.Burgum, 136 D.Forss, 138 J.Beazley, 139 P.Sharp, 140/1 H.Williams, 141 J.Beazley, 142 J.Carnie, 143 H.Williams, 144/5 R.Weir, 146, 147 J.Beazley, 148, 149, 150, 152 M.Taylor, 153 R.Weir, 154 M.Taylor, 156 M.Taylor, 157 M.Taylor, 158 M.Taylor, 159 J.Beazley.

CONTENTS

Introduction
6

Location Map
8

Index
160

INTRODUCTION

E ngland, Scotland and Wales form the largest island in Europe, with a coastline some 6000 miles (9655km) long – cliff and headland, rock and shingle, dune and marsh. Britain is a maritime country with a rich maritime heritage, and the sea has exerted a profound influence on British history and character. Harbours and coves, towns and villages all round the coast are the products of centuries of wresting a living from the sea. Britain's historic greatness rested on sea-power and sea-carried trade. The British Empire, the largest in the World's history, was controlled over vast distances by command of the sea.

The sea in its every mood, from violent storm to sullen swell to flat calm, from sparkling blue to rain-washed grey, is a familiar companion to British life. The miles of coastline run through a rich variety of scenery, each with its own magic. Along the North Devon and North Cornwall shore a line of adamantine cliffs rears up against the fury of the Atlantic, the immovable object confronting the irresistible force. Another titanic cliff barricade guards the Yorkshire coast against the North Sea. In Wales the craggy cliffs of the Lleyn Peninsula and the Pembrokeshire coast keep the Irish Sea at bay, while down Scotland's beautiful and romantic western coast the sea-lochs ripple sweetly below

Atlantic waves roll in to pound the sands of Sennen Cove on Cornwall's western tip

the mountains as the sun sinks in a blood-red glory beyond the Western Isles.

By contrast, along the flat and muddy Essex coast the sea has reached far inland to make a lonely wilderness of creeks and marshes, beloved of yachtsmen and wildflowers. Up the low-lying Suffolk shore the melancholy pebbles roar and rattle with the changing tides. A chain of delectable sandy beaches stretches down the long, smooth flank of Northumberland, and on the Lancashire coast the vast sands of Morecambe Bay glimmer under a colossal sky.

Each varied shoreline has its plant life and wildlife to discover, and coast paths conduct the walker close to much of Britain's seacoast. On the way is an engaging parade of the varying ways in which Britons have used the sea: naval bases like Plymouth, seaports from Harwich to Cardiff, venerable old trading towns like Rye and King's Lynn, picturesque little fishing harbours from Clovelly to Robin Hood's Bay with their boats and nets and wheeling gulls. There are castles and towers, lighthouses, piers and promenades. There are smart Regency seaside resorts like Brighton and Sidmouth to enjoy, with Victorian grandeur at Scarborough or Folkestone, and all the brash traditional fun of Blackpool and Skegness, Clacton and Margate.

Britain's coast has its heroes and heroines, from Sir Francis Drake and Captain Cook to Grace Darling. Writers and painters have drawn nourishment from it: Jane Austen at Lyme Regis, Tennyson on the Lincolnshire shore and the Isle of Wight, Dickens at Great Yarmouth. Generations of seamen, fishermen, boat-builders, traders, smugglers, wreckers have lived and died cheek by jowl with the beautiful and unforgiving sea, whose ebbing and flowing tides have fixed an eternal pattern, a harmony and counterpoint, at the heart of British life.

EXPLORE BRITAIN'S
COASTLINE

Location
Map

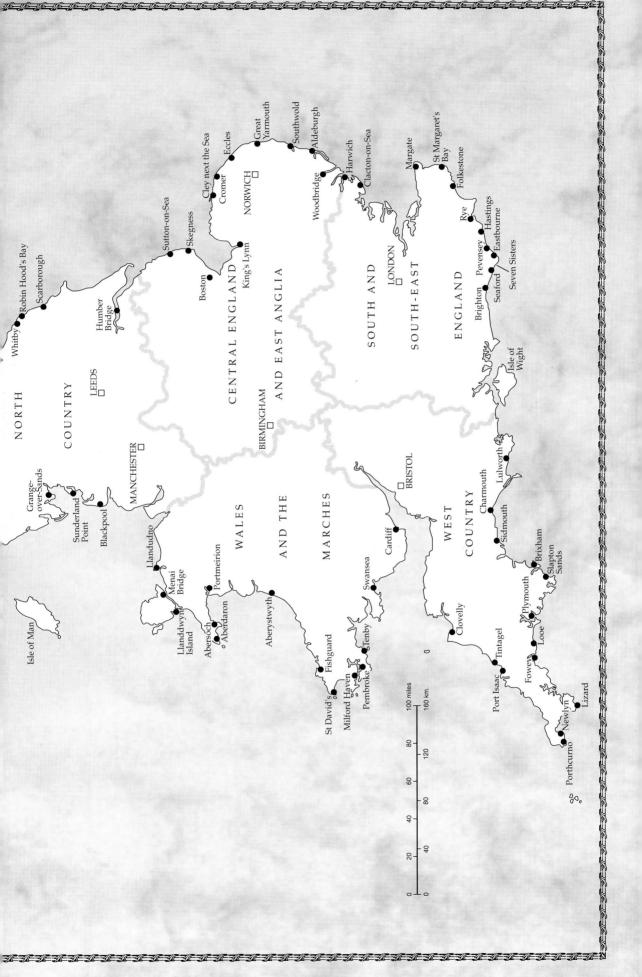

Tranquil Exmoor headlands and a blue sea at Lynmouth

WEST COUNTRY

Jutting out into the savage Atlantic Ocean, England's south-west peninsula has an ancient love-hate relationship with the sea. In quiet West Country churchyards rest countless shipwrecked seamen who met their end on cruel rocks in a welter of tumbling spars and seething foam. Cornish harbours were trading with the Continent and Ireland before the Romans came. Dark Age saints came by sea from Ireland and Wales to bring Christianity. For centuries it was quicker to travel by sea than by road, and in Devon and Cornwall this remained true until the 19th-century arrival of the railway. Nowhere in Cornwall is more than 20 miles from the sea.

The Bristol Channel coast runs south and west past Porlock Bay to the majestic sandstone cliffs of the Exmoor National Park with their deep, wooded chasms and gorges. Above Combe Martin the Great Hangman rears its ominous bulk and beyond Morte Point great gleaming stretches of sand make playgrounds at Woolacombe and Saunton. The bastion of Hartland Point confronts the full force of the Atlantic, and on down the ironbound coast past legend-haunted Tintagel, headland after headland rises above slanted, sea-beaten ribs of rock, sandy beaches, rock pools, caves and diminutive harbours with stone piers, lobster pots, fishing nets and wheeling gulls.

Approaching Land's End, the chimneys of abandoned tin mines perch precariously on cliff ledges above hidden shafts thrusting as much as a mile beneath the sea.

Turning the granite corner of Land's End, the coast starts back eastwards, rounding the Lizard with its unique serpentine rock and murderous reefs, to the winding creeks and sheltered harbours of Carrick Roads and Plymouth Sound. Old fishing villages with magical names have turned to tourism for a living – Mousehole, Marazion, Mullion, Mevagissey. The headlands were known to generations of mariners: Dodman Point, Rame Head, Bolt Head, Prawle Point, Start Point, Berry Head. The red cliffs of the South Devon coast have a warmer feel and there's a gentle climate here all year round. Looking out over Babbacombe Bay, Gerard Manley Hopkins saw a sea like silk under red cliffs with clouds rising like great white roses sunk in a blue dye.

On along the Dorset coast, the sandstone arc of Lyme Bay curves round to the long shingle bar of Chesil Bank and the limestone cliffs of the Isle of Portland, sheltering George III's favourite Weymouth. There is spectacular scenery of chalk cliffs and stacks along to the Isle of Purbeck, and the vista closes with Poole's huge natural harbour and the ranked, respectable villas of Bournemouth.

CLOVELLY
Devon

12 MILES (19 KM) WEST OF BIDEFORD

Westward Ho!
Clovelly's fine quay was built by George Cary, the 16th-century squire whose son William plays a prominent and dashing role in Charles Kingsley's *Westward Ho!* (1855). It was this popular historical novel that first marked Clovelly as a tourist attraction. Kingsley knew the village well – his father was Rector of Clovelly in the 1830s and Charles spent part of his boyhood at the rectory.

*T*umbling like a foaming cataract down the North Devon cliff, the white-washed houses of this famously picturesque village seem to stand almost on top of each other. The main street, which is cobbled with stones from the beach below, falls sharply down steps and is far too steep for cars. Donkeys used to carry visitors up and down, but nowadays you walk down on your own two feet, past cottages bright with fuchsias and nasturtiums in window boxes and hanging baskets (behind the Red Lion Inn a Land Rover lurks to take the leg-weary back to the top). At the bottom is the sturdy stone quay, where fishing boats shelter in the harbour by the former lifeboat house. The quay was built by one of the Cary squires in the 16th century and extended in the 1820s. With one of the few safe harbours on this rock-ribbed coast, Clovelly lived principally by fishing until tourism overtook it as a more profitable source of income. A visitor centre at the car park tells the story of the village's colourful past. Its old-world charm has been preserved by strong-minded squires, notably Mrs

Looking up Clovelly's cobbled main street

Christine Hamlyn, a formidable lady who inherited Clovelly and made her husband take her surname instead of the customary way round. Tiny and iron-willed, she ruled the village with passionate and tyrannical affection for 50 years from 1884 until her death in the 1930s, and the initials CH on many of the cottages are hers. The most attractive approach to Clovelly was constructed by one of her ancestors, Sir James Hamlyn Williams, between 1811

The Boat House

BOAT HOUSE
BED &
BREAKFAST
EVENING MEAL
PARKING SPACE

Fishing has taken a back seat to tourism along this coast.

and 1829, partly to provide work for Clovelly men after the Napoleonic Wars. This is the Hobby Drive, which opens off the A39 west of Bideford and makes its winding way for three miles down the cliffs through delectable woods with stunning vistas over Bideford Bay. Monuments of generations of the Carys, Hamlyns and Fanes stud the walls of the simple medieval parish church of All Saints, with its 17th-century pews, pulpit and hour-glass. Some of the pillars are of granite brought from Lundy Island, some 12 miles out in the Bristol Channel. Up in the hamlet of Higher Clovelly, on private land, are the remains of an Iron Age hill fort, which was apparently designed specially for herding cattle, perhaps gathered here for export to the Continent. Now, not far away, you can watch today's cows being milked at a working dairy farm called the Milky Way on weekends and school holdays.

The 14th-century manor house was Tintagel's post office in the 19th century

TINTAGEL
Cornwall

4 MILES (6 KM) NORTH-WEST OF CAMELFORD

Tragic Lovers

Tintagel is linked with the tale of Tristram and Iseult, an originally separate story which was drawn into the Arthurian legends. Tristram of Lyonesse was the nephew and chief champion of King Mark of Cornwall, who held court at Tintagel, and it was here that he brought the lovely Iseult from Ireland to be Mark's queen. Tragically, Tristram and Iseult fell irresistibly and hopelessly in love. In the end, when the two lovers died, the sorrowing Mark buried them both at Tintagel.

According to legend, the mighty King Arthur, 'the once and future king', was conceived at Tintagel Castle. Through the contriving of Merlin, the master magician, the beautiful Duchess Igraine of Cornwall was deceived into thinking that the man in her bed that night was her husband, the Duke – when he was really Uther Pendragon, High King of Britain. This link with the Arthurian legends inspires the all-too numerous souvenir shops in the village, but the remains of the castle are spectacularly romantic. They stand on a towering crag, high above the sea and reached by a narrow causeway and precipitous steps from the head-land, which was also fortified. Recent archaeological work here suggests that this immensely impressive place was an important royal site in the post-Roman period – the period of Arthur – and was perhaps the crowning place of the British high kings. The castle ruins themselves (English Heritage) are much later, dating from the 12th century and afterwards. The isolated church of St Merteriana and the charming medieval Old Post Office (National Trust) are well worth seeing, too. Also in the village is the weird and wonderful King Arthur's Hall, with stained-glass windows portraying the heroes of the Round Table.

PORT ISAAC
Cornwall

9 MILES (15 KM) SOUTH-WEST OF TINTAGEL

W here the stark cliffs of the North Cornwall coast stand guard against the relentless sea between Rumps Point and Tintagel Head, the little harbour of Port Isaac is sheltered by the bulk of Lobber Point. White-washed cottages crowd the narrow streets and lanes, one of which This Celtic hill fort was excavated in 1904, and pottery from shortly before the Roman period was discovered. The fort has been identified as the Castle Terrible of Thomas Malory's 15th-century epic *Morte D'Arthur* – the spot where Uther Pendragon besieged the Duke of Cornwall.

Stone and iron play harsh tunes at Port Isaac

is so cramped that it is graphically called Squeezebelly Alley. Fishing boats, nets and calling gulls lend atmosphere to a port from which Delabole slate was once shipped, before the railway arrived and took the trade away. Port Isaac was a thriving fishing harbour in the 19th century when the vast shoals of pilchard made their regular appearances along the Cornish coast. They come no more, and the little town depends on visitors for its living today. The handsome old parish church is to the south at St Endellion, and a couple of miles to the east rise the double ramparts (up to 50ft/17m wide) of Tregeare Rounds.

PENZANCE AND LAND'S END

*T*his 46-mile (74km) drive takes you around Cornwall's Land's End Peninsula at the western tip of England, an area exposed to the Atlantic yet famous for its golden beaches and its Mediterranean ambience. Ancient sites and the haunting ruins of old tin mines add to the romance of this spectacular peninsula.

>>>>

DIRECTIONS

Leave Penzance along the sea front road, following signs to Newlyn and Mousehole. At Newlyn cross the bridge and turn left, unclassified (sp. Mousehole). At Mousehole follow the narrow road down left, then right to the harbour. Turn right into Fore Street (sp. Paul, Land's End) and continue steeply to Paul. Keep ahead past the church and in ½ mile (0.8kms) turn left on to the B3315 (sp. Land's End). In 1½ miles (2.5kms) pass the turning to Lamorna Cove, then 1¼ miles (2kms) further pass the Merry Maidens stone circle. In 1½ miles (2.5kms) at a T-junction turn left (sp. Land's End, B3315) and pass the

turning to Treen village (pub). Continue on the B3315 for 3¼ miles (5kms) to a junction with the A30. Turn left (sp. Land's End). Return along the A30, go through Sennen and in 1¾ miles (2.8kms) turn left on to the B3306 (sp. St Just). After 3 miles (4.8kms) turn left on to the B3306 (sp. St Just). Three miles (4.8kms) on turn left on to the A3071 for St Just. Continue through the town and follow the B3306 (sp. St Ives) to Pendeen.

Continue for 1¼ miles (2kms) past Morvah, then follow the B3306 for 9 miles (15kms) passing the Gurnards Head Hotel and Zennor to reach St Ives. From St Ives follow the A3074 (sp. Hayle, Carbis Bay and Lelant). About ½ mile (0.8kms) beyond Lelant go forward at a roundabout, at the next take the 2nd exit to reach a large roundabout. Here, take the 3rd exit (sp. Penzance A30). In 3½ miles (5.5kms) at a roundabout, take the 2nd exit, unclassified (sp. Marazion). At the junction turn left for Marazion to view St Michael's Mount. Return, unclassified (sp. Longrock). Go ahead at the next two roundabouts, take the first exit at a large roundabout to re-enter Penzance.

Little boats shelter in the harbour at Mousehole

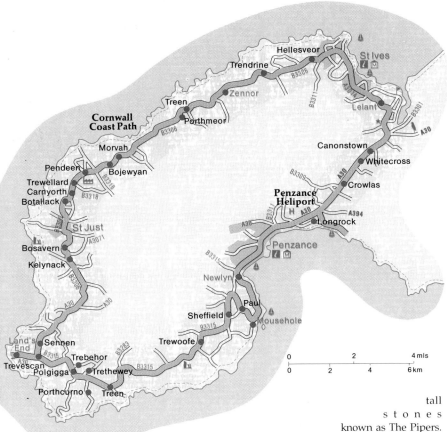

St Ives

St Ives is one of the great West Country resorts. Its appeal is based on its authentic character as a traditional fishing port, its outstanding bathing and surfing beaches and its international reputation as a centre of painting, sculpture and pottery. The focus of this artistic tradition is the Tate Gallery, St Ives, which, since 1993 has exhibited the work of such modernist St Ives painters as Peter Lanyon, Patrick Heron and Sir Terry Frost, amongst others. The workshop and studio of the celebrated sculptress Dame Barbara Hepworth is also located in the town. St Ives has numerous art and craft shops, cafés, restaurants and fine traditional pubs.

Lelant

Lying on the Hayle Estuary, the salt flats at Lelant provide the ornithologist with a rich variety of bird life. At Ryan's Field Lagoon is a new hide constructed by the RSPB, including disabled facilities, that is open to everyone. There is also a viewpoint in the grounds of Quay House. In contrast, Merlin's Magic is a theme park with a wide variety of amazing attractions that appeal to children of all ages.

>> ON THE TOUR >>

Penzance

Penzance lies on the sunny, south-facing shores of Mount's Bay. From the town's colourful harbour Chapel Street with antique and craft shops, pubs and restaurants leads to the main shopping areas of Market Jew Street and Causewayhead. Trinity House National Lighthouse Centre is near the Harbour and the Penlee House Gallery and Museum is in the attractive Penlee Gardens. The Geological Museum at St John's Hall holds one of the finest rock and mineral collections in the world. At nearby Newlyn, the Art Gallery shows international contemporary art and the best of local painting.

Mousehole

Mousehole (pronounced Mowzel) is a classic Cornish fishing village, where granite cottages and narrow cobbled streets rise in terraces from a tiny harbour. The village has a number of art and craft galleries and some fine restaurants and pubs.

The Merry Maidens

The Merry Maidens stone circle is one of Cornwall's most famous Bronze Age memorials, dating from 2400–800BC. Nineteen granite stones make up the circle. 'Merry Maidens' is a folk name derived from fanciful tales of young girls being turned to stone for dancing on the Sabbath. Nearby are two tall stones known as The Pipers. The purpose of such sites was probably cultural and religious. There is a small car park near the Merry Maidens site.

Land's End

Land's End has a unique appeal as the 'First and Last' place in England. An open, airy place perched above rugged granite cliffs, it has spectacular views of the offshore Longships Lighthouse and, on very clear days, the Isles of Scilly 28 miles (45kms) to the south-west. The area's spectacular surroundings are shown in several exhibitions and there are restaurants, cafés, gift shops and children's attractions.

St Just

St Just was once an important centre of tin and copper mining. Much of the nearby coastline, including the magnificent Cape Cornwall, belongs to the National Trust and is peppered with fascinating mining remains. There are several cafés, restaurants and traditional inns in the town's attractive Market Square. At nearby Pendeen is the Geevor Mine Heritage centre.

Zennor

Zennor is at the heart of ancient West Cornwall amidst a network of Iron Age fields. The Wayside Museum has a fascinating range of agricultural and mining artefacts. The Norman church is famed for its bench-end carving of a mermaid, derived from the legend of a young chorister whose exquisite voice so enchanted a mermaid that she spirited him away to the watery depths.

The Minack Theatre in an idyllic setting at Porthcurno

PORTHCURNO
Cornwall

3 MILES (5 KM) SOUTH-EAST OF LAND'S END

From Land's End the towering cliffs run south-east to Gwennap Head. There they turn eastwards in a succession of surf-tossed coves and commanding headlands, echoing to the rumble of the sea and the cries of gulls. Porthcurno is a particularly beautiful bay, where the first submarine cable to England across the Atlantic reached dry land over the beach. In a fabulous setting on the western headland, an amphitheatre 150 feet (50m) up the cliff, is the open-air Minack Theatre, built in the style of a classical Greek theatre. Its founder was Rowena Cade, wealthy daughter of a textile tycoon, and the theatre opened with a performance of *The Tempest* in 1932, the first in a series of successful summer seasons. On the headland at the eastern end of the bay is the Logan Rock, the most famous of the Cornish 'rocking stones' (logan is from the Cornish for 'to move'). The giant 66-ton boulder used to wobble alarmingly at a mere finger's touch – until 1824, when a naval party commanded by a Lieutenant Goldsmith went up and toppled it. Such was the uproar that the young officer was ordered to put the rock back at his own expense. It cost him a packet, and he did not get it quite right.

NEWLYN
Cornwall

IMMEDIATELY SOUTH-WEST OF PENZANCE

As celebrated for art as for fishing, Newlyn stands on Mount's Bay next door to Penzance. It is Cornwall's principal fishing port, and rows of houses look out over the harbour, with former sail lofts and fish cellars. A small harbour was built here in the 15th century and mackerel was always an important part of the catch – at one time each house would have had a pile of fish remains decaying noxiously outside the front door. When the railway arrived in 1859, fresh fish could be sent swiftly to London and the whole Cornish fishing industry was galvanised. The fish train left at 2pm every day, and long jetties were built out into the water to accommodate all the extra fishing boats. A combination of the picturesque qualities of the town and the radiantly beautiful light attracted artists from the 1880s onwards, and the Newlyn School of art developed, concentrating on painting outdoors rather than formal studio work. Its leader was Stanhope Forbes, and other artists who painted here include H S Tuke, Lamorna Birch, Norman Garstin, Frank Bramley, Laura Knight and Alfred Munnings. The town is still an important centre for artists, and their work is shown in the Newlyn Art Gallery, founded in 1895 by the Cornish philanthropist Passmore Edwards.

Fish in the Cowal
In 19th-century Cornwall the fishermen's wives used to sell the day's catch in nearby towns. The Newlyn fishwives, who were renowned for their blue-eyed good looks, were a familiar sight in the streets of Penzance, in their scarlet cloaks and big black beaver hats. They hawked their fish from baskets, or 'cowals', on their backs, suspended on a broad band that ran round each girl's hat.

Painting in Newlyn, with St Michael's Mount in the distance

THE LIZARD
Cornwall

Kynance Cove

'A steep descent leads the traveller to the shore among wild and shaggy rocks where, in the scene which opens before him, he may find the glowing fancies of a fairyland. The rocks appear as if they had been purposely grouped: and by their dark and varied colours pleasingly contrast with the light tints of the sandy beach and azure sea. The predominant colour of the serpentine is an olive green, but it is divided by waving lines of red and purple, while many of the rocks are encrusted by the yellow lichen or seamed by veins of steatite.' Murray's *Handbook for Devon and Cornwall* (1859)

The tip of the Lizard Peninsula, with its guardian lighthouse, is the furthest south you can go in England. Along the coast cliffs rising to 200ft (60m) are broken by little rocky coves, with here and there a tiny fishing village and harbour. The Lizard is known for its unique serpentine rock, predominantly green in colour. Serpentine ornaments became fashionable in Victorian times and are still made here as souvenirs. Soapstone was also extracted here. The church at Landewednack has a pulpit and lectern made of the curious stone. Much of the coast is cared for by the National Trust, including Mullion Cove, with its charming old harbour and island bird sanctuary, and Kynance Cove, a popular beauty spot known for its serpentine cliffs, caves and rock formations, where the sea spouts and hisses through a fissure called the Devil's Bellows. On the eastern side of the peninsula are the simple, white-washed cottages of Cadgwith and Coverack, the latter a celebrated smugglers' haven whose name is Cornish for 'hideaway'. Offshore lie the dreaded reefs of the Manacles, which have torn the life out of many a proud ship. Drowned seamen sleep their last sleep in the churchyard at St Keverne, whose tall spire was a vital landmark for ships in the Channel. Cornwall is well-served with tales of mermaids, and a story is told of an old man at Cury, near the Lizard, who rescued a stranded mermaid and put her back in the water. He was granted three wishes, and some years later, it is said, she returned for him, taking him down into the watery depths.

The curve of Lizard Point

*Looking north along
Kynance Cliffs on the
peninsula's western coast*

Walking the Coastal Paths

Walking is one of the most popular hobbies in Britain today, and the network of long distance paths (known colloquially as LDPs) increases each year. A significant number of these, both official routes (known as national trails) and unofficial, are set along Britain's varied coastline. An LDP is usually defined as a route of at least 20 miles (32km) that has been given a distinctive name, and for which a guide exists.

For anyone planning to walk an entire LDP, of course, careful planning, appropriate equipment, a detailed guide and some country-walking experience are also required. However, for visitors to a particular area, it is often possible to walk along just a short scenic stretch of a much longer path, following signposts and local information.

Walkers on a spectacular cliff path at Llangrannog, new New Quay

SOUTHERN COASTAL PATHS

In southern England, the South West Coast Path is a national trail, sometimes known as the South West Way, that runs for a strenuous 594 miles (956km) following – as far as possible – the very edge of the coast from Minehead in Somerset, to South Haven Point, near Poole, Dorset, through some of the finest coastal scenery in England. For much of the route it follows the path patrolled daily by the coastguard until 1913. The Saxon Shore Way is a 141 mile (225km) waymarked route along the Kent coast from Gravesend to Rye. It was along this stretch of coast that the Romans tried unsuccessfully to repulse the Saxon invaders, and four Roman forts are still to be seen. The route includes marshes, sea defences, woods, farmland and inland cliffs.

⊕

NORFOLK COAST PATH

On the east coast of England the Norfolk Coast Path is part of a national trail that runs for 93 miles (150km) from Knettishall Heath, near Thetford, through Norfolk to Holme next the Sea, then east along the coast to Cromer. There is also a south-west spur that leads from Holme next the Sea to Hunstanton. The route has also been extended along the coast, from Cromer to Great Yarmouth.

⊕

ISLAND PATHS

The Anglesey Coast Path is a 126-mile (202km) circular route around the island from the Menai Bridge, following paths and roads across beaches, marshes and cliffs. There is also a strenuous 91-mile (145km) circular route around the coast of the Isle of Man, starting at Douglas and known as Raad Ny Foillan (the Gull's Road).

⊕

NORTH OF ENGLAND

In the north of England, look out for the Langbaurgh Loop, a waymarked circular route from Saltburn-by-the-Sea, and the strenuous Northumberland Coast Walk from Alnmouth to Budle. The Cleveland Way has a 79 mile (127km) section from Saltburn to Filey, along North Yorkshire's Heritage Coast. The Northumbrian Coastline path follows a tough 61-mile (97km) route from Berwick-upon-Tweed to North Shields.

Walking near Burton Bradstock in Dorset

⊕

PEMBROKESHIRE COAST PATH

In Wales, the Pembrokeshire Coast Path is one of the best-known national trails, running for some 186 miles (299km) from Amroth along cliffs, beaches and dunes to St Dogmaels. The scenery along this footpath is beautiful and largely unspoiled, but the walking is quite strenuous in parts.

⊕

FIFE COAST WALK

In Scotland, the Fife Coast Walk is a 94-mile (152km), partly waymarked route that runs from the Forth Road Bridge around the coast to Newburgh, on the Tay estuary. This is an interesting and challenging walk that may, depending on the state of the tide, involve wading streams and making inland detours!

Manderley and Troy Town
The wealthy merchant dynasty of Rashleigh had their country house outside Fowey at Menabilly. It was later for many years the home of Daphne du Maurier, who dearly loved this part of Cornwall and put it into many of her novels and adventure stories. Menabilly itself is the 'Manderley' of *Rebecca* and also appears in *The King's General*. Another well-known literary figure, Sir Arthur Quiller-Couch (or 'Q'), lived in Fowey for more than 50 years. His house was The Haven on the esplanade and ''Troy Town' was his fictional Fowey

Fowey's lively harbour square

FOWEY
Cornwall

7 MILES (11 KM) SOUTH OF LOSTWITHIEL

The steep, narrow streets of this pleasant old town plunge down the hillside above a lovely, yacht-crowded haven on the estuary of the River Fowey. Blessed with one of the best natural harbours on the south coast, Fowey (the name is pronounced to rhyme with 'toy') was an important port in the Middle Ages, on the trade route between the Continent and Ireland which crossed Cornwall overland to the Camel estuary. Its piratical seamen, the 'Fowey Gallants', were not averse to preying on ships in the English Channel and even raiding the French coast, sometimes provoking fierce retaliation – the French came and burned the town down in 1457. In the 19th century local ships traded to the Mediterranean and across the Atlantic, and Fowey became a china clay port. The parish church of St Fimbarrus has some fine monuments to the Rashleigh family, whose 15th-century town house is now the Ship Inn. The Lugger Inn is a 17th-century hostelry, the town hall in Trafalgar Square – now housing a museum – dates from the 1790s, and there are many other interesting old buildings.

LOOE
Cornwall

7 MILES (11 KM) SOUTH OF LISKEARD

Another old port of character is set on the steep banks of the River Looe (the name rhymes with 'woo'). West Looe and East Looe, facing each other across the harbour and connected by a bridge, were separate towns until the 1880s, and each little place solemnly sent two MPs to Westminster until 1832. Cornish granite was also exported from here, including the stone to build Westminster Bridge and the Embankment in London. Most of West Looe today dates from after the arrival of the railway in 1869. East Looe is the larger and more interesting of the towns, with narrow cobbled streets and twisting alleys. Old buildings go back to the 16th century, including the Fisherman's Arms inn and the Old Guildhall, which is now a museum of local history. A popular resort with a sandy beach, East Looe developed shark fishing as a visitor attraction in the 1950s, and the Shark-sighting Club of Great Britain has its headquarters here. There are boat trips to the bird sanctuary on Looe Island, and inland up the two branches of the river. High on the cliffs to the east is the delightful Monkey Sanctuary, a colony of woolly monkeys from the Amazon rain forests which fraternise amicably with visitors.

Boats and birds bask in Looe harbour sunshine

PLYMOUTH
Devon

43 MILES (69 KM) SOUTH-WEST OF EXETER

Plymouth and the Wooden Walls

'The harbour, full of three-deckers, presents a glorious sight; which an Englishman cannot look at without feeling that inward glorying and exultation of mind, which Longinus describes as the effect of the sublime.'
Henry Matthews, *The Diary of an Invalid* (1820)

Busy today with warships, cross-Channel ferries, cargo boats, fishing smacks, yachts and assorted small craft, Plymouth Sound is a magnificent natural harbour of some 4500 acres (1800ha) in extent, formed by the junction of the rivers Tamar and Plym. An inlet on the north-east, Sutton Harbour, was the original port and the Royal Citadel (English Heritage), a fortress with walls up to 70ft (23m) high, was built to protect it in the 1660s. The Royal Naval Dockyard in the Hamoaze (the Tamar estuary) was opened in 1691. Since the 1840s it has all been protected by a colossal mile-long breakwater in the middle of the Sound, designed by John Rennie. Plymouth is one of Britain's great seafaring towns, with a history of maritime enterprise and adventure going far back into the Middle Ages. Armies were shipped over to France from here in the 14th and 15th centuries. The formidable Elizabethan seadogs – Drake, Hawkins,

Smeaton's Tower dominates Plymouth Hoe

Frobisher, Gilbert and Raleigh – all set out from Plymouth on their ventures. Sir Francis Drake sailed from here in 1577 to voyage round the world and in 1588, after calmly finishing his game of bowls on the Hoe, he sailed out of the Sound to give the Spanish Armada a drubbing. Captain Cook set off from Plymouth in the *Resolution* in 1772, to sail round the world. Targeted as a major naval base, the centre of Plymouth was heavily bombed and severely damaged in World War II, and was rebuilt during a period of singularly undistinguished architecture. The narrow streets of the Barbican area close to Sutton Harbour, however, with the fish quay and a bustling market, have retained their old character and atmosphere, and several of the merchants' and ship captains' houses of Tudor times are open to the public. The Mayflower Stone and steps here commemorate the Pilgrim Fathers, who left Plymouth for the New World in the *Mayflower*, in 1620. Overlooking the Sound from the grassy expanse of the Hoe is Smeaton's Tower, the red-and-white striped upper part of the old Eddystone lighthouse. There is a fine aquarium near by, and the City Art Gallery has a good collection of paintings by Sir Joshua Reynolds, who came from Plympton. Plymouth Dome is a 'time travel experience', with the latest technology. No visit should omit a boat trip to see the naval dockyard, and to admire the stupendous ironwork of the Royal Albert Bridge, carrying the railway line across the Tamar, with its simple, proud inscription: 'Isambard Kingdom Brunel, Engineer, 1859'.

SLAPTON SANDS
Devon

5 MILES (8 KM) SOUTH-WEST OF DARTMOUTH

Looking towards Start Point, with the sea on one side of the bar and the Ley on the other

The sea has piled up a long, straight bar of shingle that stretches north for five or six miles up the coast north of Start Point. The A379 road from Kingsbridge to Dartmouth runs along the shore over Slapton Sands – which are actually shingle, though there is sand here at low tide. On the beach grow such plants as sea radish and shore dock, and a monument recalls that this part of the South Hams area of South Devon was taken over as a rehearsal ground for American troops for the D-Day landings in 1944. Several villages were temporarily evacuated so that the soldiers could train for the Normandy beaches, and the monument was presented by the United States Army as a tribute to the local people. Behind and sheltered by the shingle ridge is the freshwater lagoon of Slapton Ley, a mile or so long, up to 10ft (3m) deep and covering about 270 acres (110ha). A nature reserve, it is rich in fish and plant life. The northern end is thick with reeds and willow. Great crested grebe, stonechat, goldcrest, coot and mallard breed here, migrant birds rest here in spring and autumn, and in winter huge flocks of gulls gather on the beach and the Ley.

BRIXHAM
Devon

5 MILES (8 KM) SOUTH OF TORQUAY

William of Orange on the waterfront, with the Golden Hind behind

Torbay or 'the English Riviera' is one of the West Country's leading tourist honeypots. At the southern end of the bay, the picturesque harbour and the steep, narrow streets of Brixham lie sheltered in the lee of Berry Head. In 1850 the town claimed to be England's leading fishing port, with more than 270 vessels – brigs, schooners and smacks – amounting to 20,000 tons of shipping. The town still has a fishing fleet, but a much smaller one. At the harbour's edge a statue of William of Orange commemorates his arrival here in 1688 on his way to be proclaimed King William III at Newton Abbot – and later in London. Nearby, a full-size replica of Sir Francis Drake's *Golden Hind*, the ship in which he sailed round the world, is moored close to the old market house. The local history is expounded in Brixham Museum, which has a special section on the coastguard service. Rev Henry Francis Lyte, who took charge of All Saints church in 1824, wrote the familiar hymn 'Abide With Me' in Brixham. A monument in the church-yard recalls 100 sailors who drowned in a terrible storm in 1866, when many boats were driven onto the rocks. The town's more modern Roman Catholic church has the curious and possibly unique distinction of having a carpark located on its roof.

Keeping It on Ice

The Great Western Railway arrived in Brixham in 1868, and gave the local fishing industry an instant boost by putting the harbour only seven hours away from London. The industry flourished on into the 20th century, but by 1939 a mere half dozen boats were left of Brixham's once proud fishing fleet. Something of a revival came in the 1960s, however, and a new fish market and deep water jetty, with its own ice-making plant, were opened in 1971.

SIDMOUTH
Devon

Fishing boats at rest on the shingle bar at Sidmouth

Sidmouth by the Sea

'At Sidmouth ... nothing intervenes between us and the coast of France. The noise of persons chattering French on the opposite coast is heard. Flat fish and mackerel have been known to leap into the drawing room!'
Sydney Smith (1831)

Dignified, charming and sedate, like a smaller and quieter Brighton, the town of Sidmouth decorously occupies a gap in the great red cliffs along the coast east of Exmouth. It is set at the point where the unfortunate River Sid, after struggling manfully for miles to reach the sea, is baulked a few yards short of its objective by a bulky bank of shingle and seems to come despondently to a halt. Striped deck-chairs stand neatly along the broad Esplanade, which was built along the front in 1837. The town, once a fishing village, developed as a seaside resort in the Regency period, when the rich and fashionable built themselves substantial 'cottages' here. It is a place of shining white terraces, elegant wrought-iron balconies with tent-shaped canopies, and flower-

packed gardens nurtured by the gentle climate, with some fine specimens of early 'Gothick' revival architecture and the fashion for the thatched and wildly picturesque *cottage orné*. Examples include the Strawberry Hill Gothick and castellated battlements of Coburg Terrace, the insanely bargeboarded Woodlands Hotel of 1815, and Beach House on the front, with its Gothicised windows and delicate ironwork. Indeed, Sidmouth claims to have England's most beautiful council house – Pauntley Cottage, with its sweetly domed roof of thatch, pointed windows and charming cottage garden. The Duke and Duchess of Kent moved here in 1819 with the baby Princess Victoria and lived in Woolbrook Cottage (now the Royal Glen Hotel), where the Duke died the

following year. The old church of St Nicholas has a striking reredos by S S Teulon, and a stained glass window presented in memory of her father by Queen Victoria in 1867. When the original church was pulled down in 1860, the local historian Peter Orlando Hutchison rescued the east end, moved it to the end of Coburg Terrace (where it still is), and lived in it. Close by is Barton Cottage, where a crippled Miss Cash lived in the 1880s and earned a living by embroidering people's names on their clothes in pink cotton on linen: hence 'Cash's name tapes', or so the story goes. To the east of the baffled River Sid, paths climb steep Salcombe Hill, with tremendous sea views. Up on top, elderly and ill-used beasts are cared for at the Donkey Sanctuary, Slade House Farm.

Beach House, built about 1790, was fashionably Gothicised in 1826

Weston to Branscombe

This is a coastal walk of approximately 6 miles (10km) along part of the East Devon footpath, with fine views of Beer Head, Portland Bill and Torbay. The scrub-covered hillside houses badgers, and the undisturbed undergrowth of the coast slips is perfect for finches and warblers. Buzzards and kestrels can also be seen.

DIRECTIONS

Having left your car at the car park in the centre of Weston, leave over the stile at he bottom of the car park towards Weston Combe. At the first fork take the left-hand path to join the coast path on Weston Cliff. Turn left beside a wonderful wildflower meadow (through which you can walk in spring and early summer) and follow the signs for Branscombe Mouth. After decending between two large mounds turn right on a track through woodland, keeping ahead until finally leaving the wood where the path forks. Take the left-hand path down steps to the car park at Branscombe Martin. Turn left along the signed path across the meadow to Branscombe village then left again. The pub is on your right.

Mason's Arms (Free House)

This is a popular, creeper-clad, 14th-century inn with a pretty terrace and colourful gardens which have ample seating. Inside the low-beamed, rambling pub, there is a massive central hearth around which chairs, cushioned wall benches and settles are arranged on the flagstones. Children are not allowed in the bar. At least six real ales, which change regularly, are always on draught. Food is served at lunchtime from noon to 2pm, and in the evening from 7 to 9pm, and there is a separate restaurant.

Turn right out of the inn through the village of pretty thatched stone cottages nestling in three deep combes. You will pass an old forge, built of wood and still working, and an old bakery that once produced bread from ovens fired by faggots, but is now a tearoom. Walk along the lane until you reach St Winifred's Church, which is well worth a visit. The church was built in the 12th century, and there still remain fragments of a medieval wall-painting, probably representing Belshazzar's Feast. Take the footpath through the churchyard, and into the woods above the combe. Turn right along the track, bearing right at a path junction. Where the footpath to Street turns off right, carry on up the track, along the lane to Berry Barton. Turn left along the quiet road for about a mile back to Weston.

Beautiful Branscombe mouth

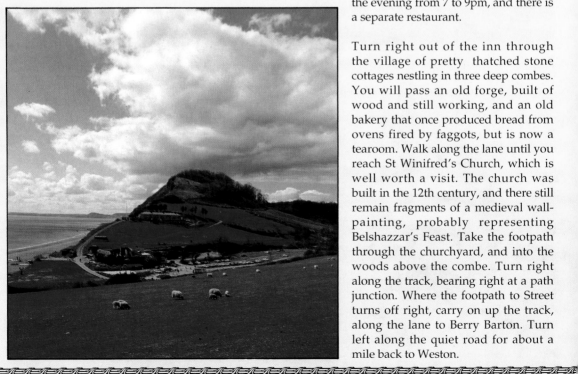

Start Point to East Prawle

This is another attractive coastal walk, approximately 6½ miles (11km) long, passing a number of coves and beaches. There is a contrasting return walk across undulating farmland with views inland of typical rolling Devon hills. Wildlife is abundant: look out for finches, pipits, cormorants, gulls, cirl buntings and colourful aromatic flowers and shrubs.

DIRECTIONS

Cars can be left at the Start Point car park (there is a small charge, and the park is supervised during the summer). Leave the car park through the white gate, immediately turn right at the signpost to Great Mattiscombe Sand and follow the path down to the coast. Turn right along the main coastal footpath and follow this to Lannacombe Beach. Continue along the coast path towards Prawle Point – the extreme southern tip of Devon. The name Prawle comes from an old Saxon word meaning 'to peep'. The rocky path soon levels onto grassland near Maelcombe House. One field after leaving the grounds of Maelcombe House follow the sign towards East Prawle, through a gate and into a lane. Turn right at the steps up a steep grassy hill, and over a wall. Turn right up the lane to join the road into the village.

At the village green there are toilets and also a café and pub with porcine names. The café is called Grunters and serves meals, snacks and take-away food (open April to October); the pub is called The Pig's Nose and is a fairly basic establishment serving one or two real ales straight from the barrel with a limited bar snack menu.

From the green, go past The Pig's Nose and follow the road round to the left before taking the first right and then right again at a phone box. Follow this lane, which becomes a track and then a path, ignoring the turn to Maelcombe House and a path left. Paths are waymarked with blue arrows on posts, and pass through two farms – Woodcombe and Higher Borough – and across fields. Remain on the path down a steep combe to a road, turn right along the road and follow signposts back to Start Point.

Prawle Point viewed from across the bay at Bolt Head

CHARMOUTH
Dorset

2 MILES (3 KM) EAST OF LYME REGIS

Charmouth Idyll

'…Charmouth, with its high grounds and extensive sweeps of country, and still more its sweet retired bay, backed by dark cliffs, where fragments of low rock among the sands make it the happiest spot for watching the flow of the tide, for sitting in unwearied contemplation.'
Jane Austen, *Persuasion* (1818)

Thatch Lodge is one of the buildings in Charmouth's conservation area

The first complete skeleton of an *ichthyosaurus*, a prehistoric reptile 21ft (7m) long, was discovered in 1811 in the Black Ven cliffs at Charmouth. This part of the coast became a paradise for fossil-hunters, but the cliffs are dangerous to climb. Now summer holidaymakers pack the beach and the grassy meadows where the little River Char makes its way to the sea. To the east the beach runs on to the towering height of Golden Cap. A flat-topped hill of bright orange sandstone, Golden Cap is a distinctive and well-named landmark, and the highest point of land along this coast, at 619 feet (189m). The hill and its surrounding area are cared for by the National Trust. The village of Charmouth is a little way inland, with a long main street that was once a Roman road. One of Charmouth's oldest buildings is the Queen's Arms, used in the Middle Ages by Cistercian monks from Forde Abbey, to which the village belonged. It is named after Catherine of Aragon, Henry VIII's first wife, who apparently stayed here on her arrival in England in 1501. Charles II stayed here, too, as a fugitive some 150 years later.

The tall man's postbox is well out of the sea's reach at Lulworth Cove.

❊

LULWORTH COVE
Dorset

5 MILES (8 KM) SOUTH OF WOOL

❊

Crowded and commercialised as it is in summer, Lulworth Cove remains beautiful. A beauty spot and geology lesson in one, the almost landlocked pool is a natural harbour, formed by the sea biting a narrow gap through the limestone cliff and then scooping out the softer rocks behind. The same process is happening next door to the west, at Stair Hole, and the cliffs all along this stretch of coast are unstable. Durdle Door is a great rock arch carved out over aeons of time by the sea, which can be seen from the coastal path above, or from one of the boats that bring visitors here in the summer. Not surprisingly, perhaps, this lonely shore was once a prime place for smuggling, and the Heritage Centre at Lulworth Cove has displays about this and other aspects of the past. The villages of West and East Lulworth and an extensive army camp lie inland. To the east is the live firing range of the Royal Armoured Corps, where much of the early development work on tanks was carried out. On non-firing days the road and marked footpaths across the range are open, and there is access to the forlorn, deserted village of Tyneham, which was evacuated during World War II when the range was extended.

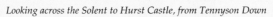

Looking across the Solent to Hurst Castle, from Tennyson Down

SOUTH AND SOUTH-EAST ENGLAND

*T*he part of England closest to the Continent has inevitably been the one most open to invasion from the rest of Europe, by both people and ideas. Julius Caesar landed at Deal in 55BC. In the following century the invading Roman legions made their base at Richborough. According to tradition, the Saxon leaders Hengist and Horsa came ashore in Pegwell Bay – there is a replica longship there now as a memorial – and so did St Augustine, coming to convert the English to Christianity in 597. William the Conqueror and his army landed further west at Pevensey in 1066.

All along England's south coast people make their living from the sea – from tourism since the 18th century, but in earlier days by fishing, legitimate trade and illegitimate smuggling. There were other ways as well. Lymington in Hampshire had a flourishing salt industry, lasting well into the 19th century, based on collecting brine from pools among the mudflats along the shore. Not far away, up the River Beaulieu, Buckler's Hard was a prosperous shipbuilding centre in the 18th century, with a good supply of timber from the New Forest.

On the other hand, the sea's vagaries can make life difficult. A build-up of shingle ended the career of Hastings as a port, and Rye and Winchelsea, once busy ports, are now miles inland up winding rivers.

Three major harbours lie next to each other along the Hampshire-Sussex coast. Southampton became Britain's leading passenger port, Portsmouth a major naval base, and the winding creeks of Chichester Harbour are a paradise for birds and small boat sailors. Bognor Regis was meant to be Hothampton, to write indelibly on the parchment of time the name of Sir Richard Hotham, a rich London hatter who spent every penny he had trying to develop the town. Further east comes a procession of fishing harbours that turned into seaside resorts: Littlehampton, Worthing, Brighton (the queen bee of them all), Eastbourne, Bexhill, Hastings, Folkestone.

Dover was always a bastion against foreign foes and its defences date from Roman times to World War II. To the north are more resorts – Ramsgate, Broadstairs, Margate – in what was once the island of Thanet. Over on the Essex shore, opposite, lies another bird and small boat paradise in a bewildering complexity of estuaries, creeks and channels where the sea thrusts its fingers deep into the coastline. Here are more tourist resorts – Southend, Clacton, Frinton, Walton – and the coast goes on to Harwich, which is all business and the ferries across the heaving North Sea.

Sunset and Evening Star
Many eminent Victorians were drawn to the Isle of Wight, among them the Poet Laureate, Alfred, Lord Tennyson, who had a house called Farringford there from the 1850s. He loved to stargaze through a telescope on his roof, walk on the down – which is now named after him – and contemplate the geology of Alum Bay. He wrote 'The Charge of the Light Brigade' and much of 'The Idylls of the King' there, entertained numerous distinguished visitors, and was made to pose for photographs by Julia Margaret Cameron, who lived at Dimbola near by. In 1888, after one of his last trips to the island on the Yarmouth ferry, he wrote 'Crossing the Bar'.

Sunset and evening star
And one clear call for me!
And may there be no moaning
*   of the bar*
When I put out to sea,

But such a tide as moving
*   seems asleep,*
Too full for sound and foam,
When that which drew from
*   out the boundless deep*
Turns again home.

ISLE OF WIGHT
Hampshire

*T*he combination of sandy beaches and chalk cliffs topped by grassy downs helped to make the Isle of Wight a magnet to visitors in the 19th century. Among them were Queen Victoria, Prince Albert and their children, who had a summer holiday home near Cowes at Osborne House (English Heritage). Their presence helped to draw the middle-classes to the island, and the house was full of happy memories for the old queen when she died there in 1901. Though the island measures only 23 miles one way and 13 the other (37km and 21km), it has a surprising variety of scenery. At the extreme western tip, the Needles are pointed stacks of white chalk, surveyed cautiously from the mainland by the Needles Old Battery (National Trust), built in 1862 against the French. Nearby Alum Bay is known for its multi-coloured cliffs. There are said to be 12 different colours and shades of sand here (the main ones are yellow-brown, white, black, green and red) and they are used in souvenirs. To the east lie Tennyson Down (National Trust), where the poet liked to stroll, and the chalk cliffs of Freshwater Bay. The south-western coast is cut by a succession of deep chasms, or 'chines', penetrating inland – the best known

The sharp-tipped Needles were once joined to the mainland and the lighthouse was built in 1859

Above the sands at Ventnor, Victorian hotels and villas climb the steep Undercliff

and most commercialised of them is Blackgang Chine. A major factor in the 19th-century development of Wight tourism was the belief that the air and climate were good for invalids, and especially consumptives. The island's senior resort is sheltered Ventnor on the south-east coast, which at one time was officially declared to be the healthiest place in England. The seawall and esplanade were built in 1848 and eager developers piled Victorian Gothic and Seaside Swiss houses on the steep rock terraces of the Undercliff, with the front doors in one street lying level with the chimneys of another. A little to the north, Shanklin is another cliff-hanging Victorian and Edwardian resort, with a sandy beach that runs on to the amusements and mile-long esplanade of Sandown. Ryde, where the Portsmouth ferries arrive, is also popular with holidaymakers. Early August regularly brings Wight into the news as the yacht-racing season peaks at Cowes, where the Royal Yacht Squadron commands the harbour with a battery of miniature brass cannon. There is a good maritime museum here, and another at Bembridge, which has a fine natural harbour. Along the north-west coast, yachts and small craft proliferate among the narrow creeks.

A TICKET TO THE
ISLE OF WIGHT

Newport

This is the capital of the Isle of Wight and its busiest town. A memorial to Princess Elizabeth, the second daughter of Charles I, can be found in the church. She died whilst in captivity in Carisbrooke Castle. The monument was commissioned by Queen Victoria. The town hall is by John Nash, who had a country retreat at nearby East Cowes Castle. A fine 3rd-century Roman villa in the town has brightly painted, reconstructed rooms.

Freshwater

Beloved by the poet Tennyson, who lived at Farringford (now a hotel). The nearby Needles Pleasure Park is a must for children.

The place that claims to have more sunshine than anywhere else in England! This 72-mile (116km) drive takes you all round the island which in parts is quite unspoilt, a place of lofty downs with pretty thatched villages, set between the Solent and the English Channel.

➤➤➤➤

DIRECTIONS

Leave Newport by the A3020 (sp. Cowes) and in ¾ mile, at the roundabout, go straight on. In a further 2 miles, at Northwood, branch left on to the B3325 then in ½ mile bear right to skirt Cowes. After another ¾ mile, at the mini-roundabout, turn left, unclassified (sp Gurnard) and in ¼ mile bear left into Church Road. Shortly, turn right into Lower Church Road and, at the next T-junction, turn left (sp. Yarmouth) to pass Gurnard Bay. In 1¼ miles turn right at a roundabout and in a further 1½ miles bear right again (sp. Yarmouth) and continue to Porchfield. Continue and, in ½ mile, bear right, then in a further ½ mile turn right (sp. Newtown). Continue past the inlet of the Newtown River and at the T-junction turn right (sp. Yarmouth). In ¾ mile, turn right

again on to the A3054 and enter Shalfleet. Follow signs to Yarmouth and cross the Yar Bridge. Stay on the A3054 and continue through Colwell. Shortly, go forward on the B3322, Alum Bay road and enter Totland. At the roundabout bear right and enter Alum Bay. Return along the same road and in ½ mile branch right, unclassified (sp. Freshwater Bay). In a further ½ mile bear right then left past the High Down Inn, and continue to Freshwater and Freshwater Bay. Here join the A3055 (sp Ventnor) and skirt Compton Bay. Continue along the coast road (sp. Ventnor) to reach Chale. Half a mile beyond the village, at the roundabout, take 2nd exit for Blackgang. Return to the roundabout and turn right with the A3055 (sp. Ventnor). Pass beneath St Catherine's Hill and continue to Niton. Here, keep left (one-way) then turn right. Continue through St Lawrence, pass the Undercliffe and Ventnor Botanic Gardens and proceed to Ventnor town centre. Leave on the A3055 (sp. Shanklin and Ryde) and soon descend to Shanklin. Follow the main road through the town to Lake. Here, pass the Stag Inn and the war memorial, bearing right to pass beneath the railway. In just over ½ mile turn right (sp. Town Centre) to

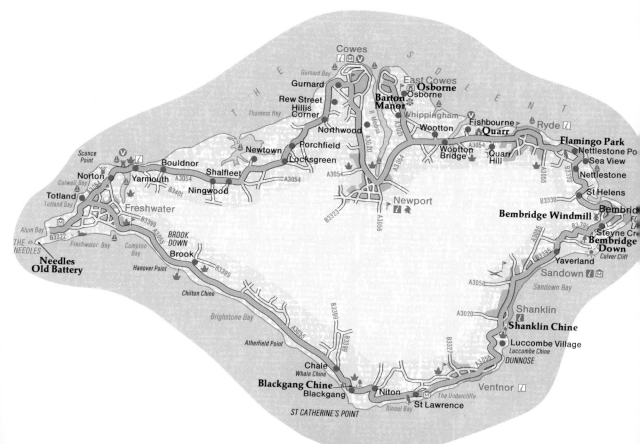

enter Sandown. Leave by the sea-front B3395 (sp. Bembridge) and in 1¼ miles, at the T-junction, turn right. Continue along the B3395 and in 1¼ miles pass Bembridge Airport. Bear left and after a further mile, at the mini-roundabout, turn left (unclassified) and continue to Bembridge. Follow the Ryde signs (B3395) to skirt Bembridge Harbour, and at St Helens, at the T-junction, turn right on to the B3330 (sp. Nettlestone). In just over ¼ mile bear sharpe left and continue to Nettlestone. Here, branch right on to the B3340 (sp. Seaview) and in almost ¼ mile further, branch right again, unclassified (sp. Sea Front). Continue to Seaview, descend the High Street, follow the Esplanade then keep forward into Bluett Avenue. Bear right then keep left along the shoreline. Continue on the coast road, veer inland then in ½ mile turn right on to the B3330. Shortly, turn right again, at a roundabout, following the A3055 soon to join the Esplanade to enter Ryde. Follow through traffic sign into town centre, then A3054 (Newport) signs to join A3054 and after 1½ miles pass through Binstead. Continue to Wootten Bridge and in 1½ miles, at the roundabout, turn right on to the A3021 (sp. East Cowes). In a further mile turn left (unclassified, sp. Royal Church of St Mildred), then in ½ mile pass the church at Whippingham. Continue to the T-junction and turn left into Victoria Grove. Join Adelaide Grove and at the end

turn left, on to the A3021 into East Cowes. Leave by the A3021 (sp. Newport, A3054). Continue on the A3021 and in ½ mile pass the road to Barton Manor Vineyard and Gardens on the left. In 1½ miles, at the roundabout, take 2nd exit A3054 and return to Newport.

>- ON THE TOUR -<

Cowes

Famous for Cowes Week, held in August, when thousands of yachtsmen – and landlubbers – flock to the town. The focal point is the Royal Yacht Squadron in West Cowes Castle, an exclusive gentleman's club founded in 1815.

Shanklin and Sandown

There is almost a continuous strip of seaside development here, with a cliff lift at Shanklin. The old village sits at the head of the chine. Keats came here for his health and stayed at what is now 76 High Street. Sandown is a mecca of seaside fun, with a zoo and a fascinating Geology Museum.

Ryde

A large town that was once a small fishing village, Ryde is famous for its entertainments, its sandy beaches and its half-mile-long pier built in 1824, which made it possible to land from large vessels.

Alum Bay, famous for its multicoloured sands

Alum Bay and the Needles
The beach at Alum Bay is reached via a continuous chairlift. From the cliffs are dramatic views of the Needles, the famous chalk stacks.

The Undercliff and Ventnor
This part of the island was developed after 1829, when the physician Sir James Clarke recommended the area for those suffering from lung disease. The Undercliff is part of a complicated series of landslips on the Gault clay between St Catherine's Point and Ventnor. Guided tours of the lighthouse at the St Catherine's Point are given during the summer months

BRIGHTON

East Sussex

48 MILES (77 KM) SOUTH OF LONDON

*I*n 1753 a certain Dr Richard Russell of Lewes moved to an obscure fishing village named Brighthelmstone on the south coast. A skilful publicist, he successfully trumpeted the medical virtues of sea air, sea bathing and even drinking sea water, judiciously mixed with milk. He also promoted a mineral spring called St Ann's Well in nearby Hove. From these bracing beginnings developed the splendidly self-indulgent acknowledged queen of British seaside resorts, with its elegant Regency terraces, squares and crescents, its grand Victorian churches, its piers and promenade and aquarium, its smart shops, restaurants and racecourse, its ice-cream parlours and whelk stalls and every variety of seaside amusement from the raffish to the exquisite. The most important single visitor in the early days was the Prince Regent, afterwards George IV. He first

Uncrowned Queen
Ever since it became fashionable, Brighton has attracted lovers. The precedent was set by the future George IV himself, who spent an idyllic summer honeymoon here with his new and entirely illegal bride, Mrs Fitzherbert. The charming Maria Anne Fitzherbert was twice widowed, and possessed of a modest fortune and an immodestly enticing figure when the Prince went through a secret marriage with her in London in 1785, in flagrant breach of the Royal Marriages Act. She took a house in Brighton, which was later rumoured to be connected to the Royal Pavilion by a secret passage, but the relationship went through many ups and downs. The Prince could not acknowledge her without losing the throne, and he finally brusquely broke off with her in 1811. She died in 1837 and lies buried near the altar of the Roman Catholic church of St John the Baptist in Kemp Town

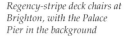

Regency-stripe deck chairs at Brighton, with the Palace Pier in the background

came here in 1783, later took a house and eventually employed the architect John Nash to build him a stately pleasure-dome, the Royal Pavilion, a wonderful oriental fantasy with dazzling Chinese-style interiors, imitation bamoo everywhere and a kitchen staffed by serried ranks of gleaming copper pans. Brighton's fashionable reputation was made, and the town expanded rapidly – eastwards to Kemp Town and to the west until it bumped into Hove. The oldest part of the town is the area called the Lanes, a warren of narrow alleys, smart boutiques and antique shops. The grandly domed Palace Pier, completed in 1901, replaced the earlier Chain Pier, which had been swept away in a ferocious storm. The West Pier of 1886 is now sadly derelict.

Among the churches, the parish church of Brighton is St Peter's, designed by Sir Charles Barry in the 1820s. The huge brick barn of St Bartholomew's in Ann Street – locally nicknamed 'Noah's Ark' – has a striking Art Nouveau Byzantine-style interior. Hove has its own sumptuous Regency squares and terraces, and an impressive Victorian legacy in the form of a working steam museum of vast hissing machines in a restored pumping station. Meanwhile the old Volk's Electric Railway rattles along the eastern part of the sea front to the enormous marina. The Hotel Metropole is the finishing point of the famous London to Brighton Veteran Car Run, an annual commemoration of the raising of the speed limit, in 1896, from 4mph to 12mph.

SEAFORD
East Sussex

3 MILES (5 KM) SOUTH-EAST OF NEWHAVEN

*T*his area of the Sussex coast is an object lesson in the waywardness of fortune. The River Ouse, which rises inland east of Horsham, flows through Lewes on its way to the sea, and originally reached it at Seaford – though it was given to changing its course through the marshes and shifting shingle banks along the shore. Seaford had a harbour and was a 'limb' or junior partner of the Cinque Port of Hastings. In the 16th century, however, a group of local landowners decided to drain the marshes and improve the navigation by cutting a canal from the wandering river to the sea at Newhaven – which gained a harbour, prospered and eventually became the ferry port for Dieppe. Seaford, on the other hand, was robbed of its harbour and was reduced to insignificance, huddled sadly around its Norman church, until the 1870s, when the Esplanade was built and it began to develop as a

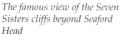

The famous view of the Seven Sisters cliffs beyond Seaford Head

modest and decorous seaside resort. The sea persecuted it every winter by flinging enormous quantities of shingle onto the front, rendering it impassible and having to be cleared at alarming expense. There is a high concrete sea wall now. On the front is the most westerly of the Martello Towers, built for coastal defence in the early 19th century, which has been turned into a small museum of local history. An enjoyable walk leads up over the heights of Seaford Head – a smaller edition of Beachy Head – and through the earthworks of an Iron Age fort to Cuckmere Haven, an old smuggling haven where the meandering River Cuckmere reluctantly consents to enter the sea. Here brandy and other contraband goods from France were unloaded in casks and bales. A shingle bank supports sea beet and sea kale, and protects a marshy lagoon where winter wildfowl feed. Beyond Cuckmere Haven lie the Seven Sisters, a tremendous wall of shining chalk, with eight (not seven) cliffs. At the western end is Haven Brow, and beyond it lie Short Brow, Rough Brow, Brass Point, Flagstaff Point, Flat Hill, Baily's Hill and finally Went Hill Brow. The western cliffs, Cuckmere Haven and the river valley form the Seven Sisters Countryside Centre which covers some 700 acres (280ha) of cliff, shingle, saltmarsh and downland, rich in plant and animal life. Gulls and jackdaws nest on the cliffs, larks and meadow pipits on the high downs. Here there is an exhibition and interpretative centre. The South Downs Way runs along the top of the cliffs.

A Death on the Cliff

In the 18th century Cuckmere Haven was used by a particularly savage gang led by a man named Stanton Collins, whose headquarters were in Alfriston at the Olde Smugglers Inn. In a notorious incident one dark night, the gang moved the lumps of chalk which the customs officers employed to follow the clifftop path, so that a revenue man slipped over the edge. He clung on by his fingertips, pleading desperately to be rescued, but the smugglers stamped on his hands and he fell to his death.

Martello Tower No 74 at Seaford houses a museum and period shops

A concert in the charming bandstand, with the pier in the distance

EASTBOURNE
East Sussex

19 MILES (31 KM) EAST OF BRIGHTON

Sheltered by the South Downs and the bulk of Beachy Head, Eastbourne basks in an exceptionally high sunshine count and a reputation for restrained middle-class charm which dates back to the mid-19th century, when it first blossomed as a seaside resort. The original village is a mile inland from the sea front, clustered round the medieval church of St Mary, and the 'bourne' or stream from which the town takes its name still runs to the and Devonshire Place, where the Duke is commemorated by a fine statue. The handsome brick church of St Saviour was built in the 1860s, and development continued to create 'the Empress of Watering Places', with grand hotels, comfortable villas, smart shops and attractive parks. The great Eugenius Birch designed the pier. At the edge of the shingle beach the promenade runs on three levels, with municipal flower gardens along the top. Cannons are ready to repel invaders on The

God gives all men all earth to love,
But, since man's heart is small,
Ordains for each one spot shall prove
Beloved over all.
Each to his choice, and I rejoice
The lot has fallen to me
In a fair ground – in a fair ground
Yea, Sussex by the sea!
Rudyard Kipling, *Sussex* (1902)

The municipal flower beds bloom brightly along the front at Eastbourne

sea concealed beneath Bourne Street. The 18th-century manor house is now the Towner Art Gallery, where a rewarding array of British art of the 19th and 20th centuries includes a major collection of work by the Eastbourne artist and designer Eric Ravilious. After centuries of inconspicuous existence, Eastbourne was developed as a resort in the 1850s, principally by the seventh Duke of Devonshire, who owned much of it. The imposing Grand Parade was laid out along the front, and terraces of houses went up in Cavendish Place Redoubt, a fortress built early in the 19th century which now houses an engagingly grotto-like aquarium and a military museum. Lifeboats from the earliest days of the service to the present are on view in the country's first lifeboat museum, opened here in 1937. Up on the sheer cliff of Beachy Head (which holds such an attraction for suicides that the Samaritans have a special sign there), the Countryside Centre focuses attention on the beauty of the downland with its rare orchids and butterflies and its superb views over the Channel.

Seaside Holidays

The holiday by the sea is a modern invention. Down into the 18th century, the sea was generally distrusted as a dangerous and disagreeable element, and few people could swim. A change of attitude stemmed more from concern with health than with fun. The beneficial effects of sea water were promoted by seaside doctors, who also blew the trumpets for sea air and invigorating breezes.

The immediate ancestor of today's seaside resort was the spa. Towns like Bath, Harrogate and Tunbridge Wells offered a combination of healthful mineral waters and smart socialising. Scarborough was a spa which happened to be by the sea, and by 1735 visitors were nervously entering the briny. The new fad spread to Brighton, which by personal appointment to the future King George IV blossomed as the smartest of resorts. His father, George III, went to Weymouth for his health in 1789 and the grateful town prospered as a resort under the mellifluous name of Melcombe Regis. Cromer was attracting rich Norwich families by this time, and Margate was a magnet for London trippers, who arrived by boat.

From the 1840s on, as the railways spread their tentacles to almost every corner of the country, visitors could reach even remote spots. Places with sandy beaches had a natural advantage, from Newquay to Ayr. So did places with a high sunshine count, such as Torquay and the Isle of Wight resorts. Landowners and developers moved to turn empty beaches and insignificant harbours

The Punch-and-Judy show shelters from the east wind at Southwold

into sources of profit: the Mostyn family at Llandudno, the Duke of Devonshire at Eastbourne, the Earl of Scarborough at Skegness.

The railways made it possible for ordinary working people to get away to the seaside for a day and, as holidays steadily lengthened, for a week or more. Resorts like Blackpool, Clacton and Skegness took the opportunity to swell out into cheerful, noisy, unabashedly vulgar magnets for the masses, with piers, funfairs, seaside rock and jellied eels, saucy postcards, fortune-telling booths,

'What the Butler Saw' machines, freak shows and variety entertainment to spice up the simple children's pleasures of paddling, sand castles, donkey rides and Punch-and-Judy.

Blackpool reached its peak number of visitors in the 1960s. It still does excellent business, but today's resorts face a challenge from changing habits: the vogue for holidays abroad and a move away from spending the whole holiday in the same place. Perhaps the traditional seaside resort will become a thing of the past, but it was fun while it lasted.

Bright stripes and gaudy colours create a cheerful holiday mood on the front at Brighton

PEVENSEY
East Sussex

4 MILES (6 KM) NORTH-EAST OF EASTBOURNE

The walls of Pevensey Castle, with the church of St Nicolas in the background

Helping Hands

Local criminals were tried in the Court House at Pevensey and there was an old tradition that a freeman of Pevensey, if condemned to death, had the right to die by drowning rather than hanging. The condemned man's hands and feet were bound and he was then thrown into the harbour. A pile of stones was kept handy to pelt him with if he was slow to succumb.

Pevensey has been fortified against invaders and marauders ever since Roman times, when the powerful stronghold of *Anderida* was constructed in the 3rd century AD as one of the forts of the Saxon Shore. After the Romans had gone, it was besieged by the Saxon warlord Aelle and his son Cissa, who took it and slaughtered everyone inside – men, women and children. The massive Roman walls are still standing up to 20ft (7m) high in places, incorporated into Pevensey Castle (English Heritage), which was built soon after the Norman Conquest by Count Robert of Mortain, half-brother of William the Conqueror. It was somewhere near this spot that William had landed with his invasion force in 1066, among sea-flooded marshes studded with small islands, or 'eyes', of which Pevensey was one. It had its own harbour until the sea receded. In 1940 the castle resumed its ancient duties when it was re-armed with a gun emplacement as part of the coastal defences against a possible German invasion – a refortification which was fortunately never tested. Close to the fortress, for protection, is the village with its tough-looking church, dedicated to St Nicolas. Other old buildings of interest include the 15th-century Mint House, which is haunted by the ghost of a woman who was starved to death there, and the Court House, with a small museum.

HASTINGS
East Sussex

32 MILES (51 KM) EAST OF BRIGHTON

*I*t was to Hastings that William the Conqueror led his army after landing at Pevensey. The town was already an important port and continued to be, as a leading Cinque Port, until stormy seas blocked the harbour with shingle. Fishing boats are still drawn up on the shingle of the Stade at the eastern end of the front, and the old town lies inland from here, in a narrow valley between the high sandstone cliffs of the West Hill and the East Hill. There's a museum of local history in the old town hall, and the Shipwreck Heritage Centre displays material from important local wrecks. A cliff railway runs up West Hill, to the remains of the Norman castle and the '1066 Story' exhibition. The extensive St Clement's Caves, partly natural and partly man-made, are open to visitors as The Smugglers Adventure. Below, the 1820s church of St Mary with its Greek Revival-style portico has been restored and is now an arts centre. Modern Hastings developed to the west – on past the Victorian pier – as a healthful seaside resort from the later 18th century on, and neighbouring St Leonard's was elegantly laid out by James Burton and his son Decimus in the 1820s and 1830s.

Unique to Hastings are the 'deezes', tall huts for storing fishermen's nets

RYE
East Sussex

*R*eposing on its hill above the surrounding levels, Rye is one of England's most beautiful and charming towns. With a wealth of half-timbered and Georgian houses, its winding cobbled streets have frequent turnings that open up freshly pleasing prospects, and its smart shops, inns, tearooms, galleries and potteries give it a thoroughly civilised air. The best approach is from the east, with a romantic view of the town across the marshes. The sea has receded and left the town high and dry two miles inland, but Rye was once one of the leading south coast ports. It provided ships for the royal fleet and fish for the royal table. It was frequently raided by the French, who burned most of the town down in 1377 – after which the English government hanged several of the leading citizens for faint-heartedness. The local history is told in the museum in the Ypres Tower, part of the 13th-century defences, and there's a fine model of the town in the heritage centre. The novelist Henry James lived at Lamb House (National Trust) before World War I, and some of his personal possessions can be seen there. The house was built in the 18th century by the Lamb family, which dominated the town at the time. A later tenant was E F Benson, author of the 'Mapp and Lucia' stories. Up on top of the hill, Rye's crowning glory is

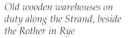

Old wooden warehouses on duty along the Strand, beside the Rother in Rye

the Norman church of St Mary, with its stumpy tower and miniature spire. The marvellous clock dates from the 1560s, and has the inscription 'For our time is a very shadow that passeth away'; two gilded cherubs strike the quarters. The stained-glass windows include designs by Burne-Jones and Christopher Webb. Rye has enough venerable inns for half a dozen ordinary towns, many of them richly equipped with smuggling tales. The doyen of them is the Mermaid Inn. The villainous Hawkhurst gang liked to take their ease here in the 18th century, with loaded pistols in full view to deter hostile enquiries. Another old hostelry, the Olde Bell, used to have a revolving cupboard for a swift getaway to the street. Down by the mouth of the River Rother a few cottages and small boats constitute Rye Harbour. This is a good birdwatching spot, here among the gravel pits where winter wildfowl flock, and paths lead along the shore to the beach at Winchelsea.

Above: Half-timbering and Georgian red brick blend in Rye's Mermaid Street

Butchers and Lambs

The Lamb family were involved in a famous murder in Rye in 1743, when a man named Breads, a butcher who owned the Flushing Inn, killed James Lamb's brother-in-law in mistake for James himself. He then went about drunkenly shouting, 'Butchers should kill lambs!' Breads was duly hanged and his body hung on a gibbet until most of the skeleton was taken by the local women and the bones boiled down to make a powerful specific against rheumatism. The skull survived and is still kept in the town hall.

RYE HARBOUR

*R*ye Harbour, adjoining the mouth of the River Rother, is a large area of stabilised shingle with a wide range of breeding birds and winter visitors, together with an interesting shingle flora. Salt-marsh, pools and grazing marsh add to the variety. Birdwatching at Rye Harbour is excellent: terns, gulls and waders breed here and a wide variety of migrant and wintering species appears in varying numbers. In all, 260 species of bird have been recorded on the reserve.

The walk is about 4¾ miles (7.5 km), and easy walking on level ground. There is no shelter, so take windproof and waterproof clothing. The car park (free) lies roughly 1½ miles (2.4 km) south-east of Rye, on the minor road signposted to Rye Harbour from the town.

❀❀❀❀

DIRECTIONS

1 From the car park walk south-east along the metalled track signposted 'No through road' which runs parallel to the River Rother. Between the river and the track is a stretch of salt-marsh comprising mainly sea purslane. Viper's bugloss, mugwort, sea-beet and sea carrot grow beside the path, together with a few clumps of salsify. The fields to the right of the path should be scanned for yellow wagtails, buntings, larks and finches. Pause at the nature reserve

sign-board and view the small pool on the right either from the path or from the small hide. Black-headed gulls and redshanks are invariably present and migrant waders can be seen in spring and autumn.

2 Continue along the path until it reaches the seafront. Scan Rye Bay for birds. At low tide, the exposed sand of Rye Bay will have gulls and waders. At high tide during the winter months, look for divers, grebes and the occasional eider duck on the water.

Retrace your steps and follow the path which heads south-west, parallel to the sea. Do not stray from the path, and keep dogs on leads. (Ignore the public footpath sign to the right unless you wish to take a short cut leading past a hide at the northern end of the Ternery Pool and back to the car park.)

The shingle on either side of the track is covered with extensive patches of sea pea, sea kale, biting stonecrop, yellow horned poppy, birdsfoot trefoil, bittersweet and the shingle form of herb Robert. Look for small copper butterflies. Ringed plovers and wheatears are frequent nesters among the shingle, which is fenced off to the right of the path in order to protect them.

3 Make a detour from the main path to the Guy Crittall hide, which overlooks the

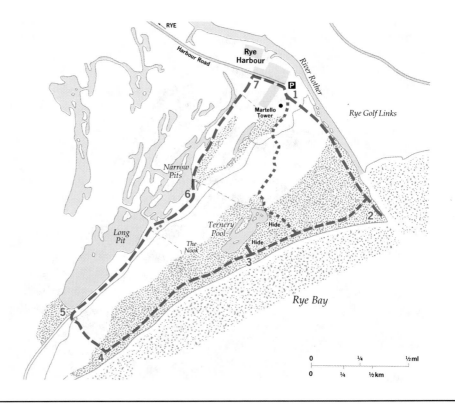

southern shore of the Ternery Pool. Shelducks, black-headed gulls, cormorants, coots, Canada geese, common terns, little grebes and oystercatchers are common in the summer months. A wide variety of waders can be seen during spring and autumn migration times. This is a good spot for unusual species: a rarely seen little egret spent several weeks here in the spring of 1990. Little terns can often be seen from the hide as they fly between fishing trips on the sea and their nests on the shingle.

4 At the reserve sign-board and map, turn right. The path is on shingle at first, but then follows a raised earth bank between two fields. Scan the fields for migrant birds and look for small skippers, gatekeepers and meadow brown butterflies, and plants including black horehound, burdock and pineapple mayweed beside the path.

5 At the footpath sign, turn right along a well-defined track and walk along the southern edge of the Long Pit. Look for gulls, grebes, cormorants and wildfowl on the water. Flocks of sparrows feed in the field to the right of the path and a few reed warblers sing from the overgrown drainage ditches. Look and listen for the occasional marsh frog. This large frog was introduced to Britain from the Continent as recently as 1935 and is now found in wetland areas around Romney Marsh, where it was first released.

6 Shortly after passing some farm buildings, the path runs around the margin of a reed-filled pool on the right of the track. Continue along the path, bearing left and keeping the edge of the Narrow Pits on your left. Look and listen for marsh frogs, reed warblers and reed buntings. Swallows and martins are common over the water in later summer and autumn. Turtle doves are common in the fields and often perch in pairs on the overhead wires. The path passes through areas of recently disturbed ground where colonising plants flourish. Look for mignonette, dark mullein and poppies.

7 After passing through a cement works, the path meets the road from Rye to Rye Harbour. Turn right and walk back to the car park.

❧

A WEALTH OF BREEDING BIRDS
Disturbance affects not only the shingle flowers but nesting birds as well – little terns, oystercatchers and ringed plovers lay their well-camouflaged eggs on the ground where they are vulnerable to trampling. Fortunately, sensitive areas are fenced off and visitors are asked to remain on the paths and keep dogs on leads. The Ternery Pool – a partly flooded gravel pit –

is a focal point for nesting birds, which can be viewed from hides.

❧

MIGRANTS AND WINTER VISITORS
Outside the breeding season, birds of many different species pass through Rye Harbour, some remaining in the area for the winter. The pools and gravel pits act as focal points for a wide range of birds, especially waders, gulls and terns. Exactly which species are present varies not only from year to year but also from day to day and hour to hour, but avocets, spotted redshanks, black-tailed godwits, little stints, curlew sandpipers and green-shanks are all regular. Black terns, sometimes in small flocks, are seen in spring and autumn, and Mediterranean and little gulls are sometimes found by careful searching among the black-headed gulls.

❧

THE LITTLE TERN
This is our smallest breeding species of tern, with a length of only 9in (23cm). A summer visitor, the little tern arrives in April and departs for its wintering grounds on the African coast in September. Two or three eggs are laid in May on bare shingle or sand. Nests and incubating birds are vulnerable to attack by ground predators and disturbance by people. The nest colonies of terns – known as terneries – are now found in protected areas where wardens prevent disturbance. Rye Harbour Local Nature reserve holds one of the most important colonies in Britain.

Shingle Flora
At first glance, shingle appears to be so inhospitable that it is a wonder any plant can grow on it. However, a wide range of species thrives in this habitat, many of them never found anywhere else. These are specialist plants – species that can cope with the shifting, well-drained pebbles and the salt-laden environment. On the walk, look for yellow horned poppy, sea kale, sea pea, sea mayweed, sea rocket, haresfoot clover and biting stonecrop beside the waymarked paths. Where the shingle grades into salt-marsh and grazing meadow, slender hare's-ear and least lettuce are occasionally found. Disturbance and trampling are a major threat to shingle plants, and Rye Harbour is now one of the few areas in southern England where the whole range of characteristic species can be seen.

An old windmill on the marshes at Rye

Something fresh and local: a fishmonger's in Old High Street

An Island No Longer

Linking Britain to the Continent physically for the first time since the English Channel was formed some 9500 years ago, the Channel Tunnel – actually three tunnels – is one of the 20th century's most exciting engineering achievements. The idea was far from new, and had been suggested in France well over a hundred years ago. A French engineer presented Napoleon Bonaparte with a plan for a tunnel to accommodate horse-drawn carriages, but the English had reason to distrust Napoleon's motives. Work on a tunnel eventually began from both ends in 1877, but was halted after an outcry in England. Digging the present tunnel began in 1986, and the French and English tunnelling parties met and joined hands beneath the Channel on 1 December 1990. On that day Britain ceased to be an island.

FOLKESTONE
Kent

14 MILES (23 KM) EAST OF ASHFORD

*T*he arrival of the South Eastern Railway in 1842 transformed Folkestone from a minor fishing village into a cross-Channel ferry port and one of the south coast's classier resorts. Within a year the first passenger ship had left for Boulogne, taking four hours over the journey, which meant that London-to-Paris could be done in a trifling 12 hours. William Cubitt's 19-arch brick railway viaduct, which takes passengers out to the ferries, has been hailed as the most distinguished piece of architecture in the town. Today, fairground amusements and small boats cluster close to the stone pier. A water-powered cliff lift carries visitors effortlessly up from the foreshore to the West Cliff and the lawns, flower beds and bandstands of The Leas, a spacious promenade with a Mediterranean air that is almost a mile long ('leas' is a Kentish dialect word for an open space). Handsome terraces and stately hotels gaze out loftily over the Channel in an area originally planned by Decimus Burton. The oldest part of Folkestone clambers steeply uphill immediately inland from the harbour, and the oldest street is probably the Old High Street. The medieval parish church of St Mary and St Eanswythe still contains the bones of Eanswythe, a Kentish princess who founded a nunnery here in the 7th century. The west window is a memorial to Folkestone's most famous

Cobbled and narrow, Old High Street is probably Folkestone's oldest thoroughfare

son, William Harvey, physician to both James I and Charles I, and the discoverer of the circulation of the blood, who was born in Folkestone in 1578. The nearby British Lion pub claims to be one of the oldest in England. Over to the east is the main bathing beach, East Cliff Sands, with a long stretch of open grassland above it, and three Martello towers. Folkestone Warren, now a nature reserve, is a tangled wilderness of tumbled chalk created by a landslip in 1915. Walks zigzag through what is locally known as 'Little Switzerland'. In Cheriton, on Folkestone's northern outskirts, the Eurotunnel Exhibition Centre tells you vividly – and in both English and French – everything there is to be told about the new Channel Tunnel and travelling through it in Le Shuttle. An observation tower commands a panoramic view of the site, and there is one of the largest model railway layouts in the country on display, as well as an array of technology, interactive exhibits and tunnel boring machinery of prodigious proportions.

Tall white cliffs at St Margaret's Bay guard the narrow sea-passage between England and France

ST MARGARET'S BAY
Kent

4 MILES (6 KM) NORTH-EAST OF DOVER

Steep and narrow, the road twists down to the bay between white, scrub-tangled cliffs. The terrace of the Coastguard pub is a good spot for watching the shipping in the Channel, and a nearby World War II pillbox still turns a cold stare out to sea. Because this is the nearest point to the French coast, a mere 21 miles (34km) away, it has long been a favourite spot with cross-Channel swimmers. Among the villas on the cliff are the lawns and flowerbeds of The Pines Garden, created here in 1970 to prevent the land being taken for a carpark. A statue of Sir Winston Churchill in bulldog mood by Oscar Nemon keeps watch. A most unusual feature is the grand façade of a 17th-century building from the City of London, lying on its back in the grass with flowers growing in the window spaces. Up at the top, the village of St Margaret's at Cliffe gathers round its sturdy Norman church, which is dedicated to St Margaret of Antioch. The local smug-glers used to store their tackle in the tower. The South Foreland lighthouse is open to the public on summer weekends and some weekdays, and a granite obelisk on the cliffs to the north honours the Dover Patrol which guarded the Channel throughout the two World Wars.

MARGATE
Kent

An engagingly dotty clock tower keeps a benevolent eye on Margate seafront

Margate's reputation as a breezy, boisterous, cheap and cheerful pleasure resort goes back well over 200 years. It was a Margate man, a Quaker glover named Benjamin Beale, who gave the world the bathing machine, which he invented in the 1750s. By 1775 the town marshalled 30 of them drawn up on its fine, curving beach of golden sand. London trippers used to arrive in seasick droves in sailing boats called Margate hoys, of 80 tons or so. In the 19th century these vessels were replaced by steamers, and the railway reached Margate in the 1840s. Today the seafront along Marine Terrace is alive with amusement arcades, bingo parlours, palmists, joke shops and souvenir shops, and places to buy fish and chips, ice cream, candy floss and Margate rock. The colossal amusement park has 25 acres (10ha) of rides with all the fun of the fair. The quieter and older part of the town is close to the harbour, the stone pier and the restored classical Droit House (the 'droits' were the harbour dues). There are pleasant old streets here and the local history museum is in the former town hall. Margate caves are a popular attraction, and the underground shell grotto on Grotto Hill is a remarkable 18th-century folly whose walls are encrusted with thousands of sea-shells.

CLACTON-ON-SEA
Essex

13 MILES (21 KM) SOUTH-EAST OF COLCHESTER

'Oh, I do like to be beside the seaside,
Yes, I do like to be beside the sea!'
Music hall song from the late 19th century

*E*ssex's answer to Margate, out of sight across the Thames estuary, is crowded with all the accustomed seaside attractions and pastimes, from old-fashioned donkey rides on the beach, putting greens and boat trips, to up-to-the-minute discos, nightspots and karaoke, with amusement arcades, ballrooms, fairground rides, a roller skating rink and the 'Living Ocean' aquarium on the pier, a naturist beach and attractive public gardens along the low cliff top above the foreshore. The Princes Theatre and the West Cliff Theatre present star entertainment, there are sightseeing flights from Clacton airstrip and family fun at Magic City – with holograms, a crazy house and an eerie shadow room as well as a much-needed bar and lounge for the grown-ups to retreat to. With all this activity it is hard to believe that only a hundred years ago there was nothing much here except a couple of Martello towers. Inland, the village of Great Clacton dozed around its medieval church and peaceable inns, the inhabitants occasionally walking the mile to the seashore for a swim. In the 1860s, however, land here went up for sale and a brand-new resort was planned. The prime mover was a railway promoter named Peter

The 1870s pier at Clacton has been extended several times

Schuyler Bruff, and he was backed by the Woolwich Steam Packet Company, which already ran regular services from London to Harwich and Ipswich, and saw prospects of profit. The virgin town was to have a pier – essential for landing the steamer passengers – a hotel and lodging houses, a promenade along the front with pleasure gardens and villas, a library and a bazaar. The stumpy little pier – later considerably extended – opened in 1871. At that point in the young resort's life there were two donkeys on the beach, two bathing huts and a few horse-drawn bathing machines, but the Royal Hotel opened in the following year, and the new church of St Paul's in 1875. In 1882 the Great Eastern Railway steamed in and by the time Peter Schuyler Bruff died in 1900, his fledgling had become one of the country's most popular resorts. In his 'Buildings of England' series, Sir Nikolaus Pevsner recommended Clacton-on-Sea as an excellent place to study Victorian suburban architecture. The Moot House is a mock medieval building constructed of genuine 15th-century barn timbers. Further east along the coast, Frinton-on-Sea was developed in the 1890s, and prides itself on its quiet superiority to the brashness of its older sister.

The war memorial rises among the semi-tropical gardens on the front

High and dry on the sands at Wells-next-the-Sea

EAST ANGLIA AND LINCOLNSHIRE

Startling contrasts characterise England's eastern coast: lonely shingle beaches under huge skies, where the grey waves clatter the pebbles in a melancholy receding roar; vast acres of low-lying marshes and dunes, penetrated by muddy straggling creeks, carpeted by sea lavender, echoing to the cries of birds; bucket-and-spade, seaside-rock, penny-in-the-slot resorts echoing to the patter of bingo-callers.

Much of this coast is a battleground between human beings and the sea. The sea has scored some dramatic victories. On the Suffolk coast, most of the prosperous town of Dunwich has vanished into the ocean – churches, houses, wharves and all. It is said the church bells can still be heard sometimes, pealing mournfully in the deep. Along the North Norfolk shore, on the other hand, and round the edge of the Wash, centuries of patient effort have won territory from the sea by piling up massive earth embankments and draining the land behind.

Up the Suffolk coast from Felixstowe, opposite Harwich, long banks of shingle line a bleak, solitary shoreline studded with empty Martello towers and teeming bird sanctuaries. At Minsmere the reed-fringed lagoons, heaths and woods of the RSPB reserve shelter avocet, marsh harrier and nightingale. Suffolk was a leading fishing county in its day, its boats bringing back herring and mackerel from the North Sea and cod from the Grand Banks, and across the Norfolk border, Great Yarmouth (there is no Little Yarmouth) was once the herring capital of Northern Europe. In the 19th century it turned round to discover the possibilities of the sandy beaches at its back, and developed into East Anglia's biggest pleasure resort.

Caravan parks and bungalows line the coast for miles north of Yarmouth, before the return of a lonelier shore, intensely vulnerable to the sea, as the scattered fragments of the church at Eccles demonstrate. These are dangerous waters for shipping, too. Exploring this coast in the 18th century, Daniel Defoe reported that half the houses were built of wood from wrecked ships.

The North Norfolk Coast is an official Area of Outstanding Natural Beauty. West of Weybourne the long shingle bank of Blakeney Spit begins and further west are sand dunes, marshes, winding creeks, small boats in inlets and swirling clouds of birds. Hunstanton is known for its high, striped cliffs, facing out over the watery wastes and flats of the Wash. King's Lynn and Boston are seasoned old ports and market towns. Northward along the Lincolnshire coast lie the golden sands, bracing air and lively amusements of Skegness and Mablethorpe, and beyond them the nature reserves leading up to the Humber.

*Cranes and ferries at rest in a
tranquil moment at Harwich*

HARWICH
Essex

16 MILES (26 KM) EAST OF COLCHESTER

Harwich is a good place for ship-watching as the big ferries and cruise ships ply in and out of Parkeston Quay to the Hook of Holland, Germany and Scandinavia. The town has a long history, which can be followed along its maritime heritage trail. It was planted on the bank of the estuary where the Stour and the Orwell flow out into the North Sea by the Earls of Norfolk in the 13th century, and over the next 200 years was used as a base for launching armies against the French. Reboubt, the recently restored fort sunk into the hillside, was built to defend against Napoleon, its guns poised to fire across the harbour entrance. The *Mayflower* was captained by a Harwich man, Christopher Jones, who lived in King's Head Street. A naval dockyard opened here in the 1660s, and one survivor of this time is the unique treadwheel crane, which was powered by men walking inside its pair of 16ft (5m) wheels. It was still in use during World War I. Another notable relic is the Electric Palace Cinema of 1911, which is the oldest unaltered purpose-built cinema in the country, now run by the Electric Palace Trust. The High and Low Lighthouses date from 1818, and the church of St Nicholas, built in 1821, has unusual columns and a gallery of cast-iron.

WOODBRIDGE
Suffolk

8 MILES (13 KM) EAST OF IPSWICH

*O*ne of Suffolk's most engaging small towns climbs a steep hill above the River Deben and the quayside, bustling with boatyards and small craft as it has time out of mind. The scene is dominated by the gleaming white Tide Mill. There has been a mill here since the 12th century. This one dates from 1793, worked until 1957 and is now a museum. It is operated by tidal water, artfully trapped in a pool behind the mill and used to drive the wheel when the tide has fallen. Visitors can see it working when the tide is right. At the heart of the town, the parish church of St Mary, with its noble 108ft (33m) tower of flint and stone, and a celebrated peal of bells, stands in a churchyard of tall trees and table tombs. Close by is the 16th-century Shire Hall, in red brick with a charming, curly Dutch gable. Notable inns include the King's Head and the 16th-century Olde Bell and Steelyard, with the steelyard itself sticking out above the street. It was used for weighing wagons and could lift a load of up to 2.5 tons.

The serenely weather-boarded Tide Mill by the harbour at Woodbridge

ALDEBURGH
Suffolk

6 MILES (10 KM) SOUTH-EAST OF SAXMUNDHAM

A fisherman and his boat on the shingle at Aldeburgh, where the sea ate much of the town

The River Alde rises near Framlingham and makes its reluctant way eastwards until suddenly, within a hundred yards of the coast, it turns right and under the disapproving eye of a Martello tower wanders on to the south for another ten miles, parallel to the shore. Aldeburgh is immediately to the north of the river's right-hand bend. A minor seaside resort and fishing village, it is also a major musical centre, known since 1948 for the Aldeburgh Festival. The little half-timbered, flint-and-brick Moot Hall was built in Tudor times as the market hall, presumably in the middle of the market place. Now it stands almost on the shingle beach where the fishermen draw up their boats, and half the Tudor town has vanished into the maw of the sea. The building was heavily restored in 1854, when the Jacobean-style chimneys were added. Today's town extends along the coast down to Slaughden Quay on the Alde, where yachts and small boats tie up. There was ship-building here in the 16th and 17th centuries, and much smuggling in the 18th, when it was said that the parson was the only man in Aldeburgh who was not a smuggler. As well as smugglers, this part of the Suffolk coast also attracted writers, including

Music Hath Charms
The annual Aldeburgh Festival of Music and the Arts, originally presided over by Benjamin Britten and Peter Pears, has become a prestigious occasion since its foundation in 1948. Many of Britten's operas and other works were given their first performances at the festival. Some events are held in the church, but the main concert hall is in the Maltings at Snape, a few miles inland. Britten lived in a converted windmill at Snape and wrote *Peter Grimes* there before moving to Aldeburgh in 1947.

Wilkie Collins and Edward Fitzgerald, the author of the fatalistic *Rubáiyát of Omar Khayyám* – though he was far from fatalistic when a wave invaded his bathing machine. Carlyle wrote approvingly of Aldeburgh's shingly beach and clear water, and E M Forster enjoyed the bleakness of the place. It was a broadcast talk about Aldeburgh by Forster that drew Benjamin Britten back to the area. The doyen of Aldeburgh authors, however, is George Crabbe, the poet-clergyman whose grandfather was customs collector here and who was born in the town in 1754. It was from him that Britten took the story of Peter Grimes.

There is a bust of Crabbe in the flint church of St Peter and St Paul. Strolling actors used to put on plays in the church, including quite possibly William Shakespeare himself in 1595. Crabbe preached as a curate from the elaborately carved pulpit. Benjamin Britten, who died in 1976, is buried in the churchyard here, and the stained-glass window in his memory was designed by John Piper. Elizabeth Garrett Anderson, Britain's first woman doctor and a leading campaigner for women's rights, died in 1917 and is also buried here. She grew up in Aldeburgh and succeeded her father as mayor of the town.

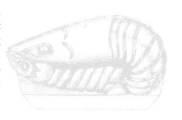

Holme-next-the-Sea to Thornham

This is an easy and interesting coastal walk of about 6 miles (10km) alongside the North Holme Nature Reserve with a break for refreshment at a pub half-way. Watch out for rare species of migratory birds.

DIRECTIONS

Leave the nature reserve car park (small charge) via the steps at the side of the information board. Turn right and follow the planked footpath through the sand dunes. The expanse of marshland on your left gives way to a view of the beach and sea, and to the right is the main area of the nature reserve. Access to this area is permitted only with a pass which can be obtained from the visitors' centre. The path enters pine woodland, the visitors' centre is clearly marked to the right. Once clear of the woods the path heads inland towards Thornham. Follow the trail along a raised bank until it meets an inlet used by yachts and other small vessels. Turn right onto the road and continue straight ahead towards the pub. The return journey can be taken along the same route or, by turning right at the visitors' centre, over the dunes and onto the beach to complete the walk.

Lifeboat Inn (Free House)

Built in the late 1500s, this pub has a well-documented history of offering a warm haven to smugglers and travellers alike. The two small bars have low ceilings, beams and dark wooden furniture, and there is a large eating area at the back, a separate restaurant, and a courtyard with many tables and a children's play area. Situated next to a campsite, this pub gets extremely busy during the summer. Greene King IPA, Abbot Ale, Woodfordes Wherry and various lagers and ciders are on draught, and excellent food is served from 12–2.15pm and from 7–10pm. The restaurant opens at 7pm, and advance booking is recommended.

Holme Nature Reserve

This is administered by the Norfolk Naturalists Trust and non-members are required to pay an entry fee. Varied habitats include dunes, salt-marsh, brackish, and fresh water pools, which make this site a paradise for a range of wildlife. Permits may be obtained to visit the Holme Bird Observatory Reserve, seven acres of pine and scrub-covered dunes where daily studies of migratory birds are carried out. There are five hides for use by visitors, a family nature trail, garden and pond.

The Suffolk shore is popular with naturalists and sailors of small boats alike, and there are many pleasant areas to explore

Dunwich Cliffs to Eastbridge

A delightful walk of approximately 5 miles (8km), which takes you through farmland, woodland and heathland starting along the seashore. The route is within Minsmere and Dunwich Heath Nature Reserves so take binoculars with you.

DIRECTIONS

Start your walk from the Coastguard Cottages on Dunwich Heath and go south along the beach or dunes to the sluice; a public viewong platform gives inland views onto the scrapes of Minsmere. Take the footpath to the south of the river, 'The New Cut', signed to Eastbridge. Follow this path, passing through two gates and a stile. This area can be muddy after rain. The footpath skirts some cottage gardens then joins the road. Turn right and a few yards along is The Eel's Foot, where food is available.

From The Eel's Foot cross a bridge into woodland. The road turns sharply right, beside a walled house. Follow the lane round to a second right-hand bend, signposted to Minsmere Nature Reserve. Take the track ahead through woodland, to open heath. Continue along the grassy path with views to the right over the marshes and sea. Walk straight across the lane, signposted right to Minsmere, and continue the path through more woodland. Just before a gate across the path, take the signed footpath to the right. Follow this path through birch wood to a stile, go straight on over the heath, before returning to the Coastguard Cottages.

Food and services also available at:

Coastguard Cottages (National Trust)
Tearooms, information, public conveniences
Minsmere Visitor Centre (RSPB)
Tearooms, information

A golden evening at Minsmere

SOUTHWOLD
Suffolk

8 MILES (13 KM) EAST OF HALESWORTH

The lighthouse and the church tower both rise 100 feet (30m) into the sky over Southwold, on its cliff above the North Sea. The gleaming white lighthouse, standing among the houses of the town, dates from the 1880s. The church is some four hundred years older, with splendid examples of Suffolk 'flushwork' – patterns made of flint and stone. It was built here to replace a previous church which had burned down, and is dedicated to St Edmund, King and Martyr, because Southwold belonged to the rich abbey of Bury St Edmunds. St Edmund was a 9th-century East Anglian king, shot to death by the Danes with arrows, like a latter-day St Sebastian, when he refused to renounce his Christian faith. The church has a fine hammerbeam roof, and the painted figures in the panels of the rood and aisle screens have been restored. The choir stalls are among the finest in the county. The ancient figure of a man-at-arms, called Southwold Jack, with bloodshot eyes and a stubbly beard, is armed with a sword and a battleaxe with which he strikes a bell to herald services or salute a bride as she arrives on her wedding day. The *Domesday Book* records a substantial tribute of herrings sent to the monks of Bury St Edmunds every year from Southwold, and Buss Creek to the north of the

Adnams' Brewery in Southwold delivers its ales in the old-fashioned way

A chorus-line of brightly painted bathing huts offers shelter from the east wind

town is named after the 'busses', or herring boats. By the end of the 16th century the town's prosperity was in danger from the same sea from which it earned its living, as the tides threatened to block the harbour mouth with shingle and a cut had to be made through it. In 1659 the town caught fire and most of it was destroyed. It was rebuilt in a style which has a distinctly Dutch flavour. The Southwold Museum on Bartholomew Green has Dutch gables and an enjoyable local collection. The first faint beginnings of a career as a seaside resort were seen in the 1820s, when the lodging houses on Centre Cliff were built – but Southwold was always a quiet place, catering for persons of refinement with its numerous open 'greens', its small houses in flint and red brick, and its Georgian inns. Six 18-pounder cannons pointing out to sea from Gun Hill were put there in the 18th century, but have never been used. The fishing harbour is to the south, at the mouth of the River Blyth.

The lighthouse rises among the houses on the cliff top

Battle in Sole Bay

In May 1672, during the wars against the Dutch, the allied English and French fleet put into Sole Bay, off Southwold, for fresh water. The commander-in-chief was the future James II, King Charles II's younger brother. In the night the Dutch navy appeared, under the great Admiral De Ruyter, and almost took the allies by surprise. Battle was joined by six o'clock in the morning, and the enemies pounded each other with terrible ferocity all day. James's flagship was so badly battered that he had to shift to another vessel, and in the evening was forced to move yet again. The *Royal James* was set alight by a fireship and blew up, and the English casualties were put at about 2500 men. Finally the Dutch withdrew, and both sides claimed the victory.

GREAT YARMOUTH
Norfolk

18 MILES (29 KM) EAST OF NORWICH

Like the Alde to the south, the River Yare heads for the sea – through the spreading sandflats and mudflats of Breydon Water – only to be deflected to the south by a narrow spit of land. It was on this peninsula that the port of Yarmouth developed, along the river and with its back turned firmly to the sea. Here the herring drifters landed their catches and the curing houses smoked the celebrated Yarmouth bloaters. Yarmouth was an active shipbuilding centre, but for centuries its prosperity rested mainly on the vast shoals of herring in the North Sea. Merchants from all over Western Europe and Scandinavia came to the medieval Free Herring Fair, which lasted for 40 days from Michaelmas. Before World War I more than a thousand fishing boats plied from Yarmouth, but overfishing eventually took its toll and the port turned to servicing North Sea oil and gas operations. There are also regular ferries to Holland, for Yarmouth is 20 miles (32km) nearer to Rotterdam than it is to London. Running inland from the quayside were the old, cramped alleys called the Rows, so narrow that a special horse-drawn vehicle called a troll cart,12 feet (4m) long and only 3 feet (1m) wide, was developed for

moving goods in the town. In 1804 they were numbered, from Row 1 to Row 145. Yarmouth was badly damaged by bombing during World War II, but parts of the Rows survived, and the Old Merchant's House and Row 111 Houses (English Heritage) are open to the public. Sections of the medieval town walls also survive, and along the river quays are examples of merchants' houses from Tudor to Victorian times, including the grand 18th-century mansion of John Andrews, the herring king, which later became the Customs House. The 13th-century Tollhouse, with its dungeons, is a museum of local history, and the Elizabethan House is now a museum of 19th-century home life. Yarmouth today is Norfolk's largest town and East Anglia's most popular seaside resort. It turned round to face the sea in the 19th century, to exploit its miles of sandy beach. The two piers date from the 1850s, and the 'Northern Margate' is fully equipped with amusement arcades, funfair rides, bowling greens, seafront gardens and lively entertainment. The Maritime Museum for East Anglia, in a former home for shipwrecked seamen, deals with the area's maritime past, and a statue of Britannia crowns the 144ft (44m) Nelson's Monument.

At Home in a Boat
Charles Dickens visited Yarmouth in 1848, and the town appears in scenes in *David Copperfield* (which came out in the following year), among them the dramatic shipwreck in which the villain, Steerforth, loses his life. Earlier in the story, Peggotty, the young David's nursemaid, takes him to her Yarmouth home in a superannuated boat with a door and windows cut in the sides and an iron funnel sticking out for a chimney. This delightful home has a strong fishy smell from the the lobsters and crabs in the outhouse, 'in a state of wonderful conglomeration with one another'.

Two faces of Yarmouth – left, the sturdy south gate of the old town wall, and below, colourful holiday activity on the sands beside the Britannia Pier

Defeated by the sea: the remains of the church at Eccles.

❊

ECCLES
Norfolk

2 MILES (3 KM) NORTH OF LESSINGHAM

❊

The village's name probably comes from the Latin word for a church, *ecclesia*, and it is thought that a church may have been constructed here originally far back in Roman times, soon after Constantine the Great's edict of toleration in AD313. This stretch of the Norfolk coast with its flat, sandy shore is particularly at risk from the sea, which invaded it regularly all through the 17th and 18th centuries. Defences were built of faggots, stones and clay, but it was not enough to save Eccles. The ruthless sea finally claimed the old village and its church of St Mary a hundred years ago. By 1858 the high tides swirled almost up to the tower of the church, which was partly buried in sand. In January 1895 a great storm finally destroyed the church completely, and all that is left now are tumbled boulders of flint masonry, lying on the beach as melancholy fragments of a lost past. The sand dunes above the beach have been planted with marram grass, to knot the dunes into a natural sea wall as protection against further encroachment by the waves. Behind this uncertain barrier are the few bungalows and beach chalets of present-day Eccles on Sea.

CROMER
Norfolk

21 MILES (34 KM) NORTH OF NORWICH

In 1779 a bathing machine was advertised at Cromer, and soon the rich Norwich banking families of Gurney and Barclay and their Quaker relations began to take holidays here, and to rent or buy houses. The resort developed further in the 19th century. The sandy beach was an attraction, and so (it was said) were 'the simple manners of the inhabitants', the fact that the sun could be seen both rising and setting in the sea, and the local dressed crab. It was a place for gentlefolk, and there was opposition when the railway arrived in 1877. Hotels and lodging houses now proliferated, the journalist Clement Scott publicised this stretch of coast as 'Poppyland', and a new pier and bandstand were built in the 1900s. The earlier Cromer was a fishing village which took the place of an earlier one still, called Shibden, that was consumed by the sea. The impressive church of St Peter and St Paul, whose 160ft (49m) tower is much Norfolk's tallest, was built in the 14th century. Nearby cottages have been turned into a museum of the area's history and natural history. There is a lifeboat museum, too, and a richly old-fashioned seaside follies show still packs them in at the pier theatre through the summertime.

'You should have gone to Cromer, my dear, if you went anywhere. Perry was a week at Cromer once, and he holds it to be the best of all the sea-bathing places. A fine open sea, he says, and very pure air.'
Jane Austen, *Emma* (1815)

The county's highest church tower soars up behind Cromer's seafront

CLEY MARSHES &
BLAKENEY POINT

Visitors to Cley

In addition to its human visitors, Cley plays host to large numbers of migrant birds during spring and autumn. Many of these are common species but birds like white-rumped sandpiper, slender-billed gull and rock sparrow are just some of the mouth-watering species that have turned up in the past few years. Cley is also Britain's most legendary site for vagrant birds, because of its position, protruding into the North Sea.

This attractive walk is approximately 3 miles (4.8km), or up to 7 miles (11 km) for the longer route. The walking is generally level, but with some shingle to negotiate, especially on the Blakeney Point section. The walk begins at The Eye car park, north of Cley village, along a side-road towards the sea wall. Cley Marshes, a block of reed-beds, lagoons and pools is exceptionally good for wading birds and other marshland specialities. The coast is also renowned for its migrants in spring and, especially, in autumn. Blakeney Point is famous for rare migrants and good for sea views and salt-marsh.

❋❋❋❋

DIRECTIONS

1 At the western side of The Eye car park, above the road-end, is a grassy bank with a path along the top. This is the West Bank, separating the reclaimed marsh from the saltings. Turn left along the path and follow it towards Cley village.

The well-preserved windmill is Cley's most distinctive feature. The muddy creeks of the salt-marsh are hidden beneath a quilt of sea purslane. This stretches as far as the eye can see to the west, framed on one side by the wooded rise around Blakeney church and on the other by the long shingle ridge of Blakeney Point. The building just visible along the Point is called the Watch House, but is known to most birdwatchers as Half-way House.

Continue along the West Bank. The mournful cries of wading birds such as

redshanks, greenshanks, curlews and grey plovers ring around the marshes all the time. Waders evolved these contact-calls to carry across open spaces, and the sounds resonate wonderfully.

The West Bank follows the road, with a narrow ribbon of reeds between the two. Opposite the small pool and sluice-gate it is a good idea to descend and follow the road, but if you have boots you can carry on a little further, until the bank angles westwards, then drop down to the road. The pool sometimes holds a few ducks, and the bushes beside it always seem to attract one or two autumn migrants such as barred and icterine warblers.

2 Turn left (away from the village) where the beach road meets the main coast road. Cars are not usually travelling fast, but take care and try to keep on the grass verge.

It is easy to be distracted by birds over the marshes to your left, but the views are poor at first because the road is barely higher than the reeds. A path above a car park on the right leads up to the Norfolk Naturalists Trust visitor centre, from where a permit may be bought to use the hides dotted around the marsh, which is well worth while. Some birds, such as passage warblers, crakes and rails, and the nesting avocets, are only seen properly by entering the reserve

Continue along the roadside. Off the road are several public hides which give better views over the marshes. Carter's

Looking back across the creek towards Cley village

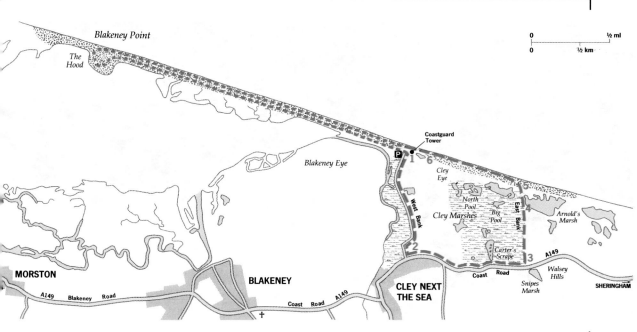

Scrape is one of the larger areas of mud and open water which is good for passage waders (ruffs, greenshanks etc.) and marsh terns if there are any about. After ¾ mile (1.2km) of road-walking you approach a scrub-covered hillside (Walsey Hills) with a reed-fringed pool (Snipes Marsh) on the right. For many years Walsey has been the site of a bird-ringing station and observatory, now run by the Norfolk Ornithological Association.

3 There is a small car park on the left side of the road, just before Snipes Marsh, and next to it is another grassy bank leading towards the sea. This is the East Bank – one of the best-known birdwatching spots in Britain. Walk along the path on the top of the bank.

To the right are grazing marshes, to the left is the Naturalists Trust reserve, of reed-beds and associated drains and channels. Many people walk straight along the East Bank, to reach either the reserve hides or the sea wall, but one of the most successful strategies can be to sit for a while in the grass and wait for birds to fly over. They always do; anything from bitterns to black terns, depending on the time of year. Even in mid-summer there are bearded tits, bitterns and harriers in the reed-beds. Drinker-moth caterpillars, cinnabar and burnet moths may share the grassy bank with you.

4 Towards the end of the East Bank pass Arnold's Marsh, on the right. This National Trust property used to be one of the best bird-watching places before the creation of all the other lagoons and scrapes, and it still attracts good numbers of wildfowl and waders.

5 At the end of the East Bank turn left and walk either along the top of the sea wall or at its base. The sea is sometimes worth watching for shearwaters, skuas etc, but it is less tiring to walk close to the marsh where the shingle is firmer underfoot.

6 Continue along the sea wall, towards the coastguard tower, passing a stile to the Naturalists Trust hide and a small brackish pool with a wartime pillbox beside it. This unattractive little pool has provided a haven for phalaropes and other storm-driven vagrants, and there are often one or two gulls, terns and plovers around it. **Return to The Eye car park.**

7 The second, optional part of the walk now leads west along Blakeney Point. To walk the 8 miles (13km) to the end of the Point and back needs considerable time and energy and is only recommended if you are fit and motivated. (A 1½–2 hour boat trip from Blakeney to Morston Quay is an enjoyable alternative in the summer, to see the tern colonies and the seals.) The Hood – about half-way along the Point – is as far as you really need to go.

The shingle ridge, colonised by yellow horned poppy, sea kale and spurrey, is the first landfall for birds on the move. When the winds have been in the east but the weather has deteriorated, thousands of migrants reach the beach in an exhausted state. Long-eared owls, woodcocks, wrynecks and a variety of other species can then be found here, drugged by tiredness and reluctant to fly. The scraps of cover sometimes carry hundreds of blackcaps, robins, goldcrests or redwings. In the winter there are usually a few snow buntings, shore larks or Lapland buntings about.

Return from The Hood along the landward side of the ridge; a path between the shingle and the mud offers an easier return route back to The Eye.

A 'First' for Conservation

To the east of the village lies a great bed of reeds with brackish and freshwater lagoons. Designated Britain's first Local Nature Reserve in 1926, a further need for protection for the birds of Cley was realised – initially to stop the shooting of rare species for collections, and now from the hoards of birdwatchers who flock here each year.

The Autumn Migration

August brings waders from the Arctic, September produces falls of wrynecks and other 'European migrants heading south, as well as seabirds passing along the coast, and there is a special buzz of excitement in October as waifs and strays from Siberia make their first landfall.

Apart from the excitement of autumn, the best time to visit Cley is probably in late May or June, when avocets are nest-building, bitterns are booming, and terns and waders will be passing up and down the shore.

CLEY NEXT THE SEA
Norfolk

4 MILES (6 KM) NORTH-WEST OF HOLT

The name is pronounced to rhyme with 'why' and it is not next to the sea any more, and has not been since the reclaiming of marshland for pasture in the 17th century left it a mile or so inland. In earlier days Cley was an important port at the mouth of the River Gleven, ranking second only to King's Lynn on this coast. Wool and later cloth was exported to the Netherlands, and the boats brought Dutch tiles back. There is still a small quay on the Gleven, but Cley's most notable feature today is the tremendous 18th-century windmill, with its sturdy brick tower, soaring white sails and conical wooden cap. One of the most photographed windmills in the country, it has been turned into a

Blakeney Point

A minor road runs northwards from Cley through the marshes to Cley Eye on the coast. From here there is a walk of three miles or so over the narrow shingle spit to the nature reserve at Blakeney Point, which belongs to the National Trust. It is a place of lonely and eerie beauty, a magnet to both botanists and birdwatchers, with its mudflats and saltmarshes , sandy hillocks and hollows, and spreading lawns of sea lavender. There's a colony of seals here in winter, terns innumerable nesting in summer with oystercatchers, redshank and other birds, and migrants coming through in spring and autumn. Blakeney Point can also be reached by boat from Blakeney Quay or Marston.

Cottages, hollyhocks and a burgeoning garden at Cley

Kippers being smoked in obedient rows at Cley

The Whalebone House has inset panels of flints in whalebone frames

guesthouse offering both bed and breakfast and self-catering holidays. Among attractive houses of flint and red brick in the village is the unusual Whalebone House, with panels of flint in the walls framed by whalebones. To the south, where the old harbour stood, the church of St Margaret is one of Norfolk's finest, rebuilt on a grand scale in the 14th century and a witness to Cley's prosperity at that time. The Black Death in the 1340s caused the money to run short, and so there is a much smaller chancel than the ample nave might lead you to expect. The two-storey 15th-century porch has fantastic battlements and a fan-vaulted roof, whose bosses are carved with angels and flowers and a woman throwing her distaff at a fox to scare it away from her chickens. The church has numerous fine brasses, including those of John Symonds and his wife in their burial shrouds, with the ominous words 'Now Thus', and their eight children. The transepts have been in ruins since Tudor days. Cley is on the part of the North Norfolk coast known to geologists as the North Alluvial Plain, a strip of land along the sea's edge, not more than 2 miles (3km) deep and built up over the last thousand years by sediment brought down by the rivers. Local landowners and farmers helped to create it by building walls and digging ditches to transform the salt-marshes into pastureland. The landscape mingles cattle pasture with saltmarshes through which creeks wind their way muddily to the sea among banks of shingle and sand. Birds haunt the area in multitudes, and almost the entire coastline is protected by nature reserves.

Birds of the Coast

*B*oth for scenic beauty and for wildlife interest, the British coastline is outstanding. It has everything from towering cliffs to shallow estuaries, shingle beaches and sand dunes. The variety and richness in both habitat and wildlife is often stunning and, whatever the season, there is always something to see. Many of Britain's best sites for birdwatching are on the coast, including the Farne Islands, and the RSPB reserves at Minsmere on the Suffolk coast, Titchwell in Norfolk, and Leighton Moss in Lancashire.

A young guillemot chick – these birds learn to fly by jumping from their cliff ledge straight into the sea

Their distinctive wedge-shaped bills make eiders one of the most easily identified ducks around the British coastline

From April until July, the cliffs of Britain are home to vast numbers of breeding seabirds, particularly to the north and west – a notable exception is Bempton Cliffs on the east coast, famous for its nesting gannets. Watch a seabird colony for even a short time and it soon becomes apparent that each species has its own special nesting requirements. Razor-bills prefer crevices and boulders close to the sea; shags and fulmars nest on broad ledges; while kittiwakes and guillemots are often densely packed on narrow ledges overhanging

sheer drops. Puffins dig burrows into the grassy slopes higher up the cliffs, while herring gulls and lesser black-backed gulls are found in loose colonies among the tussocks of vegetation.

Estuaries and mudflats, which are found all around this coast, provide wonderful opportunities for birdwatching throughout the year. The estuaries are important staging posts for migrants, and from autumn to spring vast numbers of migrant birds may be seen enjoying these rich feeding grounds. One of the most conspicuous birds of the coast is the redshank. Often called 'the sentinels of the marsh', these red-legged waders are alert and quick to utter their alarm call. This brings potential danger to the attention of other wading birds such as dunlins, ringed plovers, grey plovers, knots, curlews and godwits. Shelducks are conspicuous mudflat inhabitants,

Male and female shelducks share a bright, distinctive plumage – here an attacking bird with head held low is chasing off an intruder (see also right, above)

Left, a shelduck in flight, showing clearly its striking markings

Beaches and sand dunes, especially in southern Britain, suffer more than most habitats from human disturbance. Nesting birds also suffer, and it is only in certain protected areas in England that terns, oystercatchers, ringed plovers and black-headed gulls can rest in peace. Further north in Britain the beaches are less disturbed and you are more likely to encounter nesting birds. Always be on the lookout for signs of alarmed or distressed birds in these areas during the breeding season.

together with teal and wigeon. In some areas they feed alongside Brent geese, which are winter visitors to the south- and east-coast estuaries from their winter breeding grounds in the high Arctic. All these birds visit the estuaries to feed: huge concentrations of invertebrate life – molluscs and crustaceans in particular – live in the surface layers of the mud.

Above: fulmars, a familiar sight around Britain's coastal cliffs, are some of the longest lived seabirds, sometimes reaching 40 years or more

Left: if fulmars are the longest-lived, kittiwakes must be the noisiest of seabirds, nesting in vast colonies on sheer cliffsides

Below: oystercatchers, recognised from a distance by their striking black and white plumage and brilliant orange bill, have a distinctive call – a sharp 'klee-eep'

The most photogenic object in Lynn is the Custom House of 1683

KING'S LYNN
Norfolk

39 MILES (63 KM) WEST OF NORWICH

The civic treasures of Lynn can be admired in the 15th-century, chequered flintwork Trinity Guildhall: royal charters from 1204, regalia, maces, the superb King John loving cup. Known as Bishop's Lynn until Henry VIII confiscated it from the Bishop of Norwich, this old port on the Great Ouse, 3 miles (5km) inland from the Wash, is a place of character and charm despite the attentions of post-war planners. It grew around not one, but two market places, each close to the river and each with a noble medieval church. St Margaret's in the Saturday Market is famous for its elaborate 14th-century brasses, Baroque pulpit and 18th-century organ case. To the north is the Tuesday Market with St Nicholas's Church and St George's Guildhall (National Trust), another 15th-century edifice in chequered flint, now used as a theatre and the headquarters of Lynn's annual festival. Between the two, on the quay, is the graceful old Custom House. The Queen Street Museum displays Lynn's history and daily life from the 12th century to the 20th. Lynn Museum itself deals with regional history and wildlife, and there is a museum of the local fishing industry at True's Yard.

BOSTON
Lincolnshire

28 MILES (45 KM) SOUTH-EAST OF LINCOLN

Visible for miles around across the flat fen country is the oddly nicknamed Boston Stump, the majestic and far from stumpy tower of St Botolph's Church. Rising 272 feet (83m) high and crowned with a beautiful octagonal lantern, it commands sweeping views, as far as Lincoln in clear weather. Attached to it is one of England's largest parish churches, dating from the 14th century and a splendid testimony to the town's wealth in the Middle Ages as a port exporting wool and cloth to the Netherlands. Inside the church are misericords carved with grotesque scenes, brasses, effigies and monuments. The south-west chapel was restored in 1857 by the citizens of Boston, Massachusetts, in memory of John Cotton, a former vicar here who became a leading 17th-century Puritan divine in America. The attractive town stands on the River Witham, a little way inland from the Wash. The river had silted up badly by the 16th century, but was cleared again by 18th-century improvements. The busiest port in this part of Lincolnshire, it is also the market town of a rich farming region. The 18th-century Corporation Buildings and the later Assembly Rooms dignify the market place. In the Guildhall stand the cells in which the original Pilgrim Fathers were incarcerated in 1607.

St Botolph's Town!
Far over leagues of land
And leagues of sea looks forth
* its noble tower,*
And far around the chiming
* bells are heard:*
So may that sacred name for
* ever stand*
A landmark, and a symbol of
* the power*
That lies concentrated in a
* single word.*
Longfellow, *Boston* (1876)

Serene above the Witham, Boston Stump has been a landmark for travellers, sailors and aviators for centuries

SKEGNESS
Lincolnshire

19 MILES (31 KM) NORTH OF BOSTON

Long-Lived Old Salt

Skegness's famous symbol of the Jolly Fisherman, with his boots and heavy jersey, pipe clutched firmly in mouth, arms outspread and scarf blowing in the breeze, came from a painting by an artist named John Hassall, which the Great Northern Railway bought for £12 in 1908. That would be well over £500 today, but it was still a good investment. The Fisherman has been promoting Skegness ever since, and there are two statues of him in the town.

Bright and breezy: a helter-skelter and a carousel wait for the day to start at Skegness

'Skegness is SO Bracing', the railway posters used to say. The former fishing village was turned into a seaside resort by the local landowner, the ninth Earl of Scarborough, who in the 1870s succeeded in persuading the Great Northern Railway to run its line on from Wainfleet to the coast. The new resort's broad, tree-lined streets and comfortable Victorian villas were planned to attract middle-class customers, but in fact the railway brought holidaymakers in thousands from the Midlands industrial towns. Today Skegness's miles of golden sand are backed by acres of flower-packed gardens, while 25,000 coloured light bulbs glitter along the front at night. Funfair rides, TV-personality entertainment, discos, boating lakes and a model village add to the fun, and the country's first Butlin's holiday camp has been transformed into the huge Funcoast World leisure and water park. There is stock car racing at Skegness Stadium, and pleasure flights from the aerodrome. The Natureland zoo, with its giant aquarium, rescues orphaned seal pups. Church Farm Museum evokes life on a typical small farm at the turn of the century. To the south are the dunes and salt-marshes of the Gibraltar Point nature reserve.

Carousel horses of blinding opulence, at rest in a Skegness funfair

SUTTON ON SEA
Lincolnshire

2 MILES (3 KM) SOUTH OF MABLETHORPE

High tides and winds of hurricane strength joined forces in 1953 to cause flooding and havoc along the east coast. Sutton on Sea had to be evacuated, and afterwards the sea walls were strenghened. The sea is an old enemy here, and when the tide is low the stumps of trees, about 4500 years old, can be seen among the

next door. 'Peaceful' and 'unhurried' are the gentle adjectives chosen by the promotion leaflets, and the town relies on its sandy beach, pleasure gardens, paddling pool and bowling green to attract the type of visitor it prefers. For more vigorous entertainment – dancing, amusement arcades, a seafront fairground and the illuminations at night, Mablethorpe is handy. The

Lincolnshire Sands
'To watch the crisping ripples on the beach,
And tender curving lines of creamy spray.'
Tennyson, *The Lotus Eaters* (1832)

breakers – the remains of a forest swallowed by the ocean. The parish church vanished into the sea in the 16th century and the present one, built in 1818, was placed well back from high water. Sutton is the quiet, decorous cousin of noisier Mablethorpe

Animal Gardens care for injured seals and seabirds, and displays monkeys, owls, llamas and other animals. Mablethorpe began to attract visitors late in the 18th century, and Tennyson spent boyhood holidays here, exploring the miles of sandy beaches and dunes.

Hoofbeats along the broad and sandy shore at Sutton

Lobster pots piled high in Runswick Bay

NORTH COUNTRY

By virtue of geography, England's northern coasts were exposed to invasion and influence from Scandinavia. The Angles from southern Denmark established the kingdom of Northumbria, which had its capital at Bamburgh in the 7th century, while from the 8th century the Vikings harried and plundered the eastern shore. Lindisfarne went up in flames in 793, but where Vikings raided, Vikings settled. Scarborough has a Scandinavian name and Whitby's streets are 'gates', Danish-style.

Going north from the Humber, the sea greedily laps the low coast of Holderness and tears at the mighty bastion of Flamborough Head, with its dizzying chalk cliffs and stacks, caves and arches. North of Scarborough, the Cleveland Way footpath runs close to a wall of high cliffs along the coast, above rocky coves inaccessible except from the sea and picturesque fishing villages clinging for dear life to vertical ravines. Boulby Head, north of Staithes, is eastern England's highest sea cliff some 660 feet (201m) high.

In dramatic contrast, from Teesdale all the way to the Tyne the shoreline is scarred and blackened by heavy industry. Coal mines, steelworks, oil refineries, chemical plants and smoking power stations create a landscape that in its way is grimly impressive. Yet even here there are holiday resorts where sparkling waves foam onto golden sands, like those at Redcar and South Shields.

North up the Northumberland coast lies an officially designated Area of Outstanding Natural Beauty. Miles of sandy beaches and lonely dunes stretch enticingly past Dunstanburgh Castle, sprawled on its rock like a lion in the sun, past the teeming bird-roosts of the Farne Islands, frowning Bamburgh on its black crag, and the ancient island sanctity of Lindisfarne on the way to the Scots Border.

Over on the other side of England, the north-west coast, too, was raided and settled by the Norsemen, who conquered the Isle of Man. The remote Cumbrian coast, cut off inland by the mountains of the Lake District, has few natural harbours, but Workington and Whitehaven were developed as industrial ports in the 17th and 18th centuries.

To the south, past the Sellafield nuclear power station, the Furness Peninsula shelters the 120 square miles (310 sq km) of Morecambe Bay, where at low tide armies of birds feed on glistening sandflats and seaweed-draped rocks under a gigantic sky. South again is the flat land of the Fylde Peninsula, where a few 18th-century visitors enjoyed miles of empty, sandy beach. Today Blackpool Tower, probably the most instantly recognised construction on the entire British coastline, presides over the North's liveliest popular resort.

HUMBER BRIDGE
East Yorkshire/Lincolnshire

5 MILES (8 KM) WEST OF HULL

Swooping over the flat landscape and the rolling waters of the estuary for over 1¼ miles (2km) the graceful suspension bridge was designed by the London engineering firm of Freeman, Fox and Partners. It took eight years to complete, and when it was opened by the Queen in 1981, its single central span was the longest in the world at 4626 feet (1410m). The structure contains 470,000 tons of concrete, and its twin 533 feet (152m) towers support massive cables in which there are altogether 44,000 miles (70,700km) of wire – enough to go round the world one and a half times. The four-lane road deck is almost 100 feet (30m) above the water at high tide and there are pedestrian and cycle paths on either side. There is a spectacular view of the bridge from a special parking area off the A15 on the south side of the river, and another parking

River to Cross

The opening of the bridge put paid to the paddle steamer service across the Humber between Hull and New Holland, which itself was the successor to a long history of cross-river traffic. The Roman road from Lincoln, Ermine Street, connected with a ferry over the Humber to Brough, but even before that, rafts were plying across the river in prehistoric times. One such craft, discovered in 1974, was 40 feet (12m) long and 9 feet (3m) wide, made of heavy oak planks bound together, and would have carried heavily loaded carts over the water.

The creation of engineers rather than architects, the Humber Bridge is both functional and beautifully graceful

area on the north side. The Humber is not really a river, but the estuary of the Yorkshire Ouse and the River Trent, which drain a vast area of 9550 square miles (24,750 sq km). One of the major trade arteries in the country, it is close to a mile wide at the confluence of the two rivers, and a deepwater channel runs 22 miles (35km) from Hull to the mouth at the North Sea, where the Humber is more than 7 miles (11km) wide.

SCARBOROUGH
North Yorkshire

35 MILES (56 KM) NORTH-EAST OF YORK

The massive castle on its windswept rock commands magnificent views

Scarborough was Britain's first seaside resort, but it had a long history before that. Between the town's twin sandy bays a high cliff juts out into the North Sea. This was the site of a settlement in prehistoric times, and the Romans put a signal station here in the 4th century, part of an early-warning system against sea-raiders. On the site now is the massive medieval castle (English Heritage) with its 80ft (24m) keep, outer walls and towers. The fortress withstood many sieges and was shelled from the sea during World War I. George Fox, the founder of the Quakers, was imprisoned here in the 17th century.

The town grew up down below all this, between the castle cliff and the South Bay harbour. Narrow passageways called The Bolts served as 12th-century public lavatories, automatically flushed twice a day by the sea. When a new quay was built soon after 1300, they survived as alleys. The medieval parish church of St Mary was badly damaged during the Civil War and heavily restored in 1848; Anne Brontë's grave is in the churchyard. Scarborough became a spa after a mineral spring was discovered in the 1620s. Such disgusting tasting water must obviously be good for the human frame, and the

Swimmers frolic on Scarborough's South Bay, with the old town behind and the castle above

Nursery of Genius

The brilliant Sitwell children – Edith, Osbert and Sacheverel – spent their summers at Scarborough, where their grandparents owned Wood End. Lady Louisa Sitwell bought the house in 1870 and added to it a lavish conservatory with free-flying tropical birds. Edith Sitwell was born there in 1887, 'an exceedingly violent child', according to her mother. At the age of four, asked what she wanted to be when she grew up, she replied, 'A genius', which did not go down well. Her brother Osbert was baptised in St Mary's Church. Another famous Scarborian was the actor Charles Laughton, who was born in the Victoria Hotel, opposite the station, in 1899. He had his first stage success in Scarborough, at the old Arcadia Theatre in 1925, in *Hobson's Choice*. He loved the town and was a frequent visitor. His hotelier brother Tom assembled the Laughton Collection of British art which now graces Scarborough Art Gallery.

spring was trumpeted by the local medical men as a panacea for ailments including melancholy and hypochondria. The spa had a smart social life of balls and card parties, and early in the 18th century patients took to swimming in the sea – behaviour previously unheard of. The arrival of the railway from York in 1845 signalled a boom period for the town, and the Victorians have left a splendid legacy of hotels, houses and beautiful terraced gardens. The colossal Grand Hotel, by the great Yorkshire architect Cuthbert Brodrick, with 365 rooms on 12 floors, is now owned by the Butlin organisation. The 1860s church of St Martin on the Hill, by G F Bodley, is a treasure-house of Pre-Raphaelite work, with stained-glass by Burne-Jones, Rossetti, William Morris and Ford Madox Brown. In the Rotunda Museum of local history, opened in 1829, the original display cabinets can still be admired. Scarborough Art Gallery is in a Victorian villa of 1845, and the Wood End Museum of natural history is in the former home of the Sitwells and contains many mementos of the family. Scarborough also comes equipped with all the expected seaside entertainments, including the monster Sealife Aquarium and the Kinderland children's play park.

Narrow streets meet at Way Foot, where the fishing boats are dragged ashore

ROBIN HOOD'S BAY
North Yorkshire

6 MILES (10 KM) SOUTH-EAST OF WHITBY

The curving expanse of Robin Hood's Bay, with its sandy beaches and cliffs riddled with caves, stretches from North Cheek or Ness Point down to Ravenscar. Near the northern end is the village – often called Bay Town – diving down a steep ravine to the sea, its cottages cramped along narrow alleys and diminutive courtyards, piled so closely on top of one another that they have been compared to sand martins' nests. Constantly menaced by the sea which eats away at the cliff, the village lived for centuries by fishing, combined with the smuggling of brandy, gin, tea and silks brought surreptitiously across from Holland. The writer Leo Walmsley, who lived here from 1894 to 1913, made the most of the smuggling tradition in stories in which the village appears as 'Bramblewick'. In 1885 the railway arrived and brought a new source of income from visitors and 90 years after that a 40ft (13m) sea wall went up to keep the sea at bay. Where the connection with Robin Hood comes from is a mystery, but the name apparently goes back at the latest to 1538. According to various local stories, the doughty outlaw took his summer holidays here, or was hunted here by pursuers and escaped by dressing up as one of the fishermen, or perhaps he came here to help the monks of Whitby against the Danes.

WHITBY
North Yorkshire

The River Esk makes its way through a deep gorge to reach the sea at Whitby, where the houses of the picturesque former whaling port perch on the steep sides of the cleft. Up on the East Cliff stand the ruins of medieval Whitby Abbey (English Heritage), successor to the one founded here by St Hilda in AD657 and destroyed by the Danes some 300 years later. Near by, the parish church of St Mary has a Norman tower and a charming 18th-century interior recalling the inside of a wooden ship – it is the work of the local shipwrights. Observing a coffin being carried up the 199 steps from the town for a funeral inspired Bram Stoker to set part of *Dracula* here. (You can follow a Dracula Trail today and visit the Dracula Experience if you dare!) The great explorer James Cook learned his seamanship at Whitby, which was a flourishing whaling centre in his time. He is commemorated by a statue on the West Cliff, and the house he lived in is now a museum. There is material about him in Whitby Museum, too, with engaging collections of fossils, bygones and Whitby jet, which was fashionable for mourning jewellery in Victorian Britain.

The Norman tower of St Mary's looks out over the old town and harbour

ROBIN HOOD'S BAY

*R*obin Hood's Bay is one of the most attractive seaside villages in England, looking out over a bay cut deep into the North York Moors coastline by the North Sea. The sea continues to batter the coast, wearing it away at an estimated rate of 2 inches (5 cm) per year. The area is renowned for its fossils and is of great interest to geologists. The walk begins some 3 miles (4.8km) down the coast at Ravenscar, and is about 7½ miles (12km) long. It is mostly easy walking, with some sections near cliffs, and it can be muddy in winter. Park on the demarcated roadside verge approaching the Raven Hall Hotel.

❀❀❀❀

DIRECTIONS

1 Take the path signposted 'Cleveland Way' leading past the National Trust Coastal Centre, then turn left by a sign indicating a geological trail to reach the abandoned railway track. The sides of the railway track have been colonised by an interesting range of wild flowers, trees and shrubs. Plants like hemp agrimony and fleabane attract butterflies, and bramble and gorse patches are good places for other insects like bumble bees and beetles.

2 Follow the railway track for 3 miles (4.8 km), descending to cross roads in two places where the original railway bridges are missing. The mixture of woodland, scrub and open fields provides excellent opportunities for birdwatching, and several species of songbird can be seen along the route. Small mammals are abundant here, although not often seen; the tiniest of all, the pygmy shrew, sometimes betrays its presence by the shrill squeaking noise it makes when it meets another shrew. Foxes may be glimpsed early or late in the day.

3 When a caravan site on the left is reached, climb over the ladder-stile on the right where there is a public footpath sign. Cross the field diagonally left to a gate in the far corner, then follow the path alongside the hedge to Robin Hood's Bay.

Herring gulls are common here, but the bay may have more unusual species of birds sheltering in it or roosting on exposed rocks at low tide. Look for turnstones, purple sandpipers, oyster-catchers and redshanks on the rocks, and rock pipits on the upper shore.

4 At low tide it is possible to walk along the shore for ½ mile (800m) as far as Boggle Hole Youth Hostel. The Cleveland Way can be joined here, or you can walk along the beach for a further 500 yds (450m) or so to the next tiny inlet, where a footbridge crosses a stream. Join the main cliff path (Cleveland Way) here.

The gently shelving, rocky shore is an excellent habitat for marine life and is worth exploring at low tide. The brown seaweeds, or wracks, hide delicate creatures like beadlet anemones beneath them, and periwinkles, topshells, dogwhelks, limpets and shore crabs can all be found here. The strand line is a good place to look for empty shells and interesting seaweeds washed up from deeper water. After winter storms, many fossils will be found among the beach pebbles. (Do not hammer fossils out of the rocks and cliff-faces.)

5 At high tide do not go on to the foreshore; take the stone steps to the right at the end of the road in the village and follow the signs marked 'Cliff Path'. The path crosses the Mill Beck below the Youth Hostel and the Stoupe Beck by footbridges.

With binoculars, it should be possible to watch seabirds from breeding colonies further down the coast as they fly by to feed. Small numbers of gulls and fulmars breed here, but many of the cliffs are too unstable to provide safe nesting sites.

Robin Hood's Bay and the cliffs, seen from the aptly-named Stoney Beach

Cormorants sometimes fish close to the shore at high tide. Patches of gorse and bramble on the cliff-top provide nesting sites for stonechats and the less conspicuous whinchat, and rock pipits breed below the cliff-edge.

6 The Cleveland Way leads back to Ravenscar, running along the cliffs as far as High Scar, then turning inland in the direction of some abandoned quarries. Wheatears may be seen in more open places, especially in early summer.

7 Fork right by the signpost before the golf course and continue to the abandoned railway line and the start of the walk in Ravenscar. Green woodpeckers occasionally feed on the golf course, and kestrels are frequent visitors.

❀
A MECCA FOR GEOLOGISTS
The coastline around Robin Hood's Bay displays many interesting geological features in a relatively small area. There is a classic wave-cut platform and cliffs of glacial till. The main cliffs have been eroded by the sea to reveal a section through rocks of the Jurassic period from 160 million years ago, and a vast number of ammonites and other fossils have been found here. Ravenscar has a geological trail which explores various rock types and the old alum quarries.

The limestone beds overlie the shales and have been eroded by the sea on the foreshore to form striking mushroom-shaped 'mermaid's tables'. In the beds of sandstone there are fossilised 'ripple marks', formed when the rocks were on the bed of a shallow sea. Dinosaur footprints can be traced, although no skeletons have been found. The beds of shales are a good source of ammonites, belemnites and oysters.

Coastal erosion is still causing problems in this area, and several houses have fallen into the sea. Extensive coastal defences have been built to combat this.

❀
ALUM QUARRIES
Alum was an important chemical in the tanning and dyeing industries, and is still used as a colour fixative in dyed cloths. Huge quantities of shale were removed from the cliffs around Ravenscar in order to extract alum. In the process many fossil ichthyosaurs were uncovered, and several museums obtained good specimens. Most of the alum was loaded on to ships from Robin Hood's Bay. When the railway came in 1885 the industry was already declining, so even though the line passed through the quarries it was never used to transport alum. The National Trust, which owns the main works site at Low Peak, is consolidating the remaining structures and carrying out archaeological investigations.

Seashore Life
The submerged rock ledges stretching far out into the bay offer excellent hiding places for marine organisms, and at low tide it is possible to explore them and discover something of the life below the high-tide line. Several species of brown seaweed grow on the shore, including bladder wrack, with its gas-filled flotation bladders, and serrated wrack, with its saw-tooth edge. Beneath them live many creatures which shelter from predators or the heat of the sun when the tide is low. Gulls and wading birds visit the shore to forage among the seaweeds for small prey like tiny shrimps and crabs. Near the low-water mark are the large kelps, rarely uncovered by the tide; cormorants may be seen here when the tide is in, fishing. Storms throw large quantities of seaweed and other debris on to the strand line, where it begins to decompose. Kelp flies lay their eggs in it and these produce tiny larvae which feed on the decaying seaweed. These are an important source of food for turnstones and land birds like rock pipits and pied wagtails. Twice a day the tide rises and falls, bringing a fresh supply of food to the seashore creatures and depositing more material on the high-tide line, so this is one of the richest of wildlife habitats.

SOUTH SHIELDS
Tyne & Wear

7 MILES (11 KM) NORTH OF SUNDERLAND

Beyond the funfair's glitter are the quiet grey piers of South Shields

An unusual combination of industrial town and seaside resort, with a past going back to Roman times, South Shields began as *Arbeia*, a fort built in the 2nd century AD in a commanding position on the south bank of the River Tyne. The Roman army developed a major port here and a supply base for the troops garrisoning Hadrian's Wall. The foundations of the granaries can still be seen, the fort's imposing west gate has been reconstructed and there are impressive Roman tombstones in the site museum. In the 17th and 18th centuries South Shields was the centre of the local salt industry, with 200 salt pans heated with coal, giving off what one visitor called 'a perpetual thick nasty smoke'. The main development came in the Victorian age as simultaneously a mining town and a beach playground. The rippling waves and sandy beaches attracted holidaymakers, while miners toiled in shafts of the Westoe Colliery far out beneath the sea, and the docks were busy grimily exporting coal. To the south in Marsden Bay the sea has carved out a great rock arch in the limestone cliffs. To the west, in Jarrow, is an extraordinary survival – the little Saxon church of St Paul, which the Venerable Bede knew 1200 years ago, standing unobtrusively in the middle of a vast industrial wilderness.

FARNE ISLANDS
Northumberland

BETWEEN 2 TO 5 MILES (3–8 KM) OFF THE COAST AT BAMBURGH

A boat trip nears Staple Island with its stacks and seabirds

The Penitent Raven

'One day some ravens which had long inhabited the island were seen tearing the straw from the roof of the visitors' house and carrying it off to build their nests. The saint reproved them with a slight gesture of his right hand and told them to leave the monks' property alone. They merely scorned his command.

"In the Name of Jesus Christ, depart forthwith!" he shouted. "Do not dare remain to do more damage."

They flew off shamefacedly almost before he had finished speaking. Three days later one of a pair of them returned, and finding Cuthbert digging, stood before him, with feathers outspread and head bowed low to its feet in sign of grief. Using whatever signs it could to express contrition it very humbly asked pardon. When Cuthbert realised what it meant, he gave permission for them all to return. Back they came with a fitting gift – a lump of pig's lard.'

Venerable Bede, *Life of Cuthbert* (8th century) (trans J F Webb, Penguin Classics)

The National Trust acquired the Farne Islands in 1925, and protects them as a bird sanctuary. Farne is Celtic for 'land', and these 30 or so bits of sea-lapped dolerite rock with their stacks and cliffs can be reached by boat from Seahouses when it is not too rough. Inner Farne and Staple Island are open at limited times to visitors, who are strongly recommended to wear hats! St Aidan used to come to the islands from Lindisfarne for lonely prayer and meditation, and St Cuthbert, the Northumbrian shepherd boy who became the north of England's most admired saint, lived as a solitary for a time on Inner Farne. He built himself a hut, and there are stories of him reproving the greedy and thoughtless birds and bringing them to conduct themselves in a more Christian manner. He died on the island in AD687. A chapel there survives, built in his memory in the 14th century. Friendly grey seals breed on the islands and puffins make tunnels in the sand or take over rabbit burrows. They are called Tommy Noddies locally, because of the way their heads bob as they walk along. Other nesting birds here include petrel, guillemot, cormorant, all sorts of tern and the eider ducks, known as St Cuthbert's chicks or cuddy ducks because the saint particularly loved them.

BAMBURGH
Northumberland

5 MILES (8 KM) EAST OF BELFORD

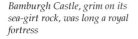
Bamburgh Castle, grim on its sea-girt rock, was long a royal fortress

Northumberland has been called 'the kingdom of castles' because of its tally of frowning and formidable strongholds, keeping watch in a debated and dangerous land. One of the most impressive of them all is Bamburgh Castle, 150 feet (46m) up on its almost vertical black crag, from which it glares forbiddingly out to sea across a broad expanse of sand. It seems entirely fitting that it should appear in the Arthurian legends as Joyous Garde, the castle of Sir Lancelot of the Lake, the greatest of the paladins of the Round Table. The outcrop on which it stands is part of the Whin Sill, the seam of dolerite rock that appears to dramatic effect along Hadrian's Wall, in the Farne Islands and on Lindisfarne. The stone keep was built in the 12th century, but much of the castle today dates from the period after 1894, when it was renovated and rebuilt by Lord Armstrong, the inventor and armaments magnate. A

Grace Darling's shrine-like tomb in Bamburgh churchyard

fine succession of rooms includes a well-stocked armoury, the King's Hall, the keep hall and the kitchens. There may well have been a Roman signal station on this vantage point. In AD547 an Anglo-Saxon king built a wooden fortress on the rock and King Oswald of Northumbria, who founded the monastery on nearby Lindisfarne in 635 made Bamburgh his capital. Later it suffered attacks by marauding Vikings, who in the 10th century destroyed it altogether. The Normans built the present keep, with a well dug down 150 feet (46m) through solid rock. A small town grew up under the castle's protection, and in the Middle Ages this boasted a Dominican friary, a market on the triangular green and fairs in honour of King Oswald and St Aidan. Aidan, of the Lindisfarne monastery, died at Bamburgh in AD651, and the church is dedicated to him. In the graveyard is the elaborate tomb of local heroine Grace Darling, and a museum in the village tells her story. Grace's father was the keeper of the Longstone Light in the Farne Islands, and one stormy night in 1838 the steamer *Forfarshire* struck on a rock. Grace and her father rowed out at peril of their lives in an open boat in huge seas to pick up survivors, not once but twice. The 22-year-old girl's courage caused a sensation and she became a national celebrity but, sadly, she died only four years later.

The Laidley Worm

An 18th-century ballad, 'The Laidley Worm of Spindlestone Heugh', tells the story of a king who married a second wife and brought her home to Bamburgh. The new wife hated her stepdaughter, Margaret, and by evil magic turned her into a 'laidley worm', or loathsome dragon, whose destroying breath devastated the whole countryside. Hearing of this when away overseas, the king's son returned to Bamburgh and went sword in hand to kill the dragon, but the monster cried out to him to kiss it three times. Bravely, he did and it changed back into his sister Margaret. The pair then turned her own spell back on the wicked stepmother and transformed her into a hideous toad, which still lurks in a cave deep beneath Bamburgh Castle.

One man and his dog in quiet contemplation of Whitehaven Harbour

WHITEHAVEN
Cumbria

7 MILES (11 KM) SOUTH OF WORKINGTON

Lightning Strike

In the small hours of 23 April 1778, Whitehaven suffered a surprise attack by John Paul Jones, the infamous marauder and captain of the ship *Ranger*. Jones had served an apprenticeship at Whitehaven and knew the port well. He and his men stole in, spiked the guns of the harbour battery and fired a ship, but the alarm was raised and they withdrew. Jones's exploits built him a heroic reputation in the United States and he was awarded a gold medal by Congress.

The first planned town created in England since the Middle Ages, Whitehaven was developed during the 17th century by three generations of the Lowther family, the great Cumbrian landowning dynasty who became Earls of Lonsdale. In 1633 it was a miserable fishing hamlet, but the Lowthers set out to exploit the coalfields on their estate here. They built a harbour and a new town which became a mining centre, with shafts excavated far out beneath the sea, and a major port, shipping coal to Ireland and the Continent and importing tobacco from America. Handsome Georgian and Victorian buildings testify to the town's prosperity, and the church of St George, designed by a mining engineer, has one of the most stunning Georgian interiors in the country: it is like being inside something made by Wedgwood. There are old quays and harbour works to be seen, and Whitehaven Museum explains the local history. Close by, to the south, rise the sandstone cliff ramparts of St Bee's Head, up to 300 feet (100m) high, with a lighthouse and wonderful sea views to the Isle of Man. There is an attendant RSPB reserve, with one of the largest seabird colonies on England's west coast, and a notable medieval priory church.

GRANGE-OVER-SANDS
Cumbria

14 MILES (23 KM) SOUTH-WEST OF KENDAL

*T*he little grey town, more a retirement community than a resort today, has its back to the Lake District and looks south over a magnificent prospect of the alluring and treacherous sands of Morecambe Bay. Once known, somewhat flatteringly, as 'Cumbria's Riviera', it has a sheltered site, a gentle climate, pleasant 19th-century hotels, and attractive gardens planted with exotic shrubs. The 'grange' in the town's name belonged to the monks of medieval Carmel Priory, who had a vineyard here and a small harbour for bringing in sea coal. As a resort, Grange was boosted by the railway from Furness, which arrived in 1857 and in characteristic Victorian style was built unhesitatingly along the seafront, between the village and the shore. The promenade along the front was built in 1904. A fashionable health spa developed on the strength of the water from St Ann's Well at Humphrey Head, a limestone headland three miles to the south, which was good for gout and the stone. There is a pleasant walk to Humphrey Head, where England's last wolf is said to have been killed (though it has been sardonically suggested that it must have gone to Grange to retire). Another enjoyable walk leads over Hampsfield Fell to Cartmel, with its impressive priory church.

The Ornamental Gardens at Grange-over-Sands are backed by a terrace of Victorian shops

Wooden Walls

*B*ritain is an island, and islands undoubtedly require boats. The first Stone
Age settlers who came across the Channel some 6000 years ago probably used
open boats of the coracle type, whose relatives can still be seen on one or two
Welsh rivers. Since those distant times, the needs of fishing, commerce,
communications, crime, defence, rescue and pleasure have governed the
evolution of a rich complexity of vessels.

Drifters were built for inshore fishing, drifting along with wind and current. The prototype of the modern deep-sea trawler is said to have been designed in the 18th century at Brixham – a two-masted sailing ship which was the forerunner of the trawling fleets of Grimsby, Hull and Aberdeen in their great days. Today's big trawlers can stay at sea for weeks on end, use sonar to locate shoals of fish and refrigerate their catches on board.

Shipyards all round the coast built boats for local needs and conditions. There were Deal galleys and Deal luggers, Polperro gaffers, Isle of Man nobbies, Yorkshire billy boys and north-eastern cobles. Trows carried cargo down the Severn and across the Bristol Channel. Ketches plying to the little stone harbours of the West Country were some of the last working sailing ships afloat. Beer luggers were South Devon beach boats, Mumbles oyster skiffs and Tenby luggers could be seen off South Wales and scaffies and fifies off the Scottish east coast. Bawleys went shrimping and oyster dredging along the Kent and Essex shores of the Thames estuary. The two-man Morecambe Bay prawners were specially designed to harvest the

*Boats on the shingle at Beer in
South Devon – a local type of
sailing lugger was developed
here*

area's most toothsome delicacy, while the Yarmouth beach yawls were among the biggest open sailing craft in Europe.

Until the 19th century, moving cargo and people by water was generally easier, quicker and cheaper than by land. Collier brigs called 'cats' hauled coal from the north-east of England down the coast to London. The Thames sailing barges with their tarry black hulls and reddish-brown sails carried corn, bricks and hay from East Anglia to London, and horse manure for fertiliser back to East Anglia again. They had flat bottoms, for shallow draught and to stay upright if grounded.

Steam power began to replace sail in the 19th century, but it was the railways that slowly strangled the coastal traffic and drove the smaller harbours into decline. A recovery came with the growth of pleasure sailing and small boat racing, which boomed after World War II.

HMS Victory at Portsmouth, one of the 'wooden walls' that defeated Napoleon

SUNDERLAND POINT
Lancashire

2 MILES (3 KM) SOUTH-WEST OF OVERTON

*F*rom the historic city of Lancaster the broad River Lune flows south through marshes towards the sea, curving past the port of Glasson Dock and leaving on its right bank the fossilised remains of the former port of Sunderland Point, before emerging into the glimmering stretches of Morecambe Bay. On land, Sunderland Point is reached by car across a causeway from the village of Overton. At high water the causeway is covered, but as the tide falls the road appears among glistening channels and shining banks of wet mud on which the birds swoop for food. Motorists not infrequently leave the crossing too late and are caught by the

tide. Sunderland Point is an isolated backwater among the marshes now, but there was once – astonishingly – a prosperous harbour here. It was the brainchild of a wealthy Quaker merchant named Robert Lawson at the end of the 17th century, and he developed it as a port for Lancaster, trading with the West Indies. He made an anchorage with a quay, and built warehouses, now converted into houses and flats, where incoming cargoes of rum, tobacco and cotton were stored. It is said that the first consignments of cotton ever to reach Britain arrived here, and a 'cotton tree' in the village is actually a kapok tree, which presumably grew from seeds

From the epitaph on
Sambo's Grave:

'...*Full many a Sandbird chirps
   upon the Sod
And many a Moonlight Elfin
   round him trips,
Full many a Summer's
   Sunbeam warms the Clod
And many a teeming Cloud
   upon him drips,
But still he sleeps –* '

*The grave of a faithful slave,
who died here thinking
himself abandoned*

Boats among the lonely marshes and flats of the Lune Estuary

The Old Bath House at Sunderland Point, which was a busy port in the early 1700s

that arrived here in a cotton bale. Lawson appropriated some of his building stone from the ruins of Cockersand Abbey, a 12th-century foundation in a hauntingly lonely situation on the opposite, southern bank of the Lune Estuary. His creation at Sunderland Point flourished for a time, but unfortunately things began to go wrong with Lawson's finances, he went bankrupt in 1728 and the port withered away. Its successor was Glasson, where a harbour was built in 1783. The most striking point of interest in today's Sunderland Point is the grave of a faithful black slave called Sambo, who was left at the inn here by his master, a West India merchant. The master intended to come back for him, but the poor slave, thinking himself abandoned, lost heart, took sick and died. Marking his grave in unconsecrated ground is a rough cross and a stone inscribed with a flowery poem, put here in 1796 to commemorate the tragedy of 60 years before. Still today, posies of wild flowers are often left at the grave.

ISLE OF MAN

30 MILES (48 KM) WEST OF ST BEES HEAD

Set in the sea about half way between England and Ireland, the island is known for its ancient Manx language and its tailless Manx cats, for a parliament much older than the one at Westminster, for its symbol of the Three Legs and for its low taxes. Towns and villages strung out along a coastline running for 90 miles (145km) and more developed as seaside resorts in the 19th century, when visitors first began to arrive in substantial numbers – drawn by the grandeur of the mountain and cliff scenery, miles of sandy beaches, rocky coves, picturesque fishing harbours and spectacular sunsets over the Irish

Sea. The capital, largest town and leading pleasure resort is Douglas, on the east coast. Essentially a Victorian town, which has kept its charming horse-drawn trams, it boasts a 2-mile seafront promenade, an opulent Edwardian theatre, casinos, discos and a lively nightlife. The famous TT motorcycle races start and finish here. The 19th-century parliament buildings house the Tynwald and the House of Keys, the Cattery naturally houses Manx cats, and the Manx Museum is a treasure-house of information about the island's rich Celtic and Viking past. The Manx Electric Railway runs north through fine coastal scenery to

The cathedral of St German was founded in the 13th century, within the shelter of Peel Castle

The best Manx kippers come from Peel, a busy fishing port on the west coast

Ramsey, a seaside resort and yachting centre on a gorgeous curving bay against a backdrop of mountains. Further on, the Ayres Nature Trail investigates the wildlife and geology of Man's northern plain and coast. Until the 1860s the capital was Castletown, on the south coast, a quaint old place where the Kings of Man lorded it in their medieval fortress of Castle Rashen, on the site of an earlier Viking stronghold. To the west is the watersports centre of Port St Mary, its harbour protected by a 1200ft (370m) breakwater. The coastal walk from here goes down to the south-west tip of the island, past the deep clifftop fissures called the Chasms, to the high bastion of Spanish Head. The island offshore, the Calf of Man (Manx National Trust) is a bird sanctuary reached by boat in calm weather from Port St Mary or Port Erin. The rare chough can be seen here, and grey seals are regular visitors to Man's shores. On the rugged west coast at Peel, where the best Manx kippers come from, a mighty fortress looms over the busy fishing harbour. Within its formidable walls are an Irish-style round tower and the shell of medieval St German's Cathedral. A spectacular Viking Festival here in July recalls Manxdom's ancient roots.

BLACKPOOL
Lancashire

15 MILES (24 KM) WEST OF PRESTON

Mr Blackpool

In 1928 a new attraction came to Blackpool with the installation in the Tower Ballroom of 'the Wonder Wurlitzer', the biggest electric organ outside America, with 15 miles (24km) of wiring and a range of magical sounds which ranged from cathedral chimes to birdsong and breaking waves. An even bigger machine replaced it in 1935, to be played for many years by Reginald Dixon, the Wurlitzer wizard, whose tune 'I Do Like to be Beside the Seaside' became familiar on radio as the signature of 'Mr Blackpool'. He gave his last concert here in 1970, to a huge audience, and he died at the age of 80 in 1985.

The North's champion brash, cheerful, noisy pleasure ground has been drawing visitors in droves for a hundred years and more. In 1900 the count was 3 million people a year. By the 1960s, when 150,000 human beings arrived expectantly in Blackpool every average summer day, the annual figure peaked at 8 million. Blackpool is still packing them in. It made its reputation as the top resort for the millhands of the booming Lancashire textile industry before World War I, but it has always kept up with the times. Its miles of inviting sands still offer safe swimming and the traditional donkey rides and Punch and Judy shows, but in case of disappointing weather an enormous indoor beach called the Sandcastle provides 300ft (90m) water chutes and wave pools. The massed amusement arcades of Britain's slot machine capital come equipped with video technology, and the Pleasure Beach funfair boasts the latest spine-chilling rides and rollercoasters. In 1990 the biggest ferris wheel in Europe, 180 feet (55m) high, opened on the central pier. The celebrated Illuminations, which clothe the front with gigantic daisy chains of glittering light on autumn nights, now have the benefits of lasers, fibre optics and computer control. Blackpool has everything. It has three piers and a 7-mile promenade, paraded by delightful electric trams. It has theatres, dancing, discos, night spots. It has ice and roller skating rinks and a waxworks. For quieter moments there is good shopping, an enjoyable collection in the Grundy Art Gallery, and the formal Italian gardens, model village and boating lake in Stanley Park. The Tower once had a zoo

(where the lion ate Albert in Stanley Holloway's comic monologue) and a circus and the world's longest bar. Opened in 1894, in the teeth of local opposition, the Tower was pre-fabricated in Manchester and brought to Blackpool by train to be assembled. Half the height of the Eiffel Tower in Paris, on which it was modelled, it stands 518 feet and 9 inches (158m) tall and there are remarkable views from the top. It was restored and reopened in 1992, with a 'dawn of time' ride through the earth's history to add to its giant aquarium and adventure playground. In 1840 there was still only a single row of cottages on Blackpool's seafront, but things changed after the railway arrived in 1846. The great surge of development came between 1870 and 1910, when the population multiplied sixfold and the major Victorian and Edwardian attractions were established – the promenade, the piers, the winter gardens, the Empress Ballroom, and of course the Tower itself. The Pleasure Beach was opened in 1890 as a place where grown-ups could recapture their childhood. They still do.

An old-fashioned treat on Blackpool's sands, with the Tower in the background

Sturdy Pembroke Castle, birthplace of Henry VII

WALES

*T*wo of Britain's most enjoyably characterful resorts are in Wales – Llandudno on the north coast and Tenby on the south. The country's steepling mountain ranges, romantic lakes and dark forests are confined in a coastline of spectacular cliffs and golden beaches that stretch from here to eternity, while along the south coast lie piquant contrasts between natural beauty and the man-made scenery of heavy industry.

From Point of Ayr, where the River Dee emerges fretfully into the Irish Sea, a procession of popular seaside resorts – Prestatyn, Rhyl, Colwyn Bay, Rhos-on-Sea – marches westwards to bow before stately Llandudno. Across the Menai Strait, the island of Anglesey (the name is said to mean 'isle of Angles', which makes no sense at all) was the original home of the Tudor dynasty, and long before that a centre of the Druids. Today it is a stronghold of the Welsh language, and so is the Lleyn Peninsula, whose craggy coast is an official Area of Outstanding Natural Beauty.

The peninsula forms the northern arm of Cardigan Bay. Tucked into the armpit, overlooking the beautiful Glaslyn Estuary, is the enchanting village of Portmeirion. To the south lies a succession of fine beaches and estuaries, interspersed with cliffs and coves, and punctuated by swimming and sailing resorts from Barmouth and Fairborne down to Tywyn,

Aberystwyth and the Georgian dignity of Aberaeron. Then from the spreading Teifi Estuary south, the Pembrokeshire Coast National Park protects 180 miles (290km) of superlative scenery, past a parade of rearing headlands – Cemaes Head, Dinas Head, Strumble Head, St David's Head – and into the sheltered calm of Milford Haven, one of the finest natural harbours on earth, with its estuaries and creeks reaching far inland. Offshore lie the bird-haunted islands of Ramsey, Skomer, Skokholm.

East of Tenby come the sandy reaches of Carmarthen Bay, with the limitless Pendine Sands where Sir Malcolm Campbell and Parry Thomas smashed land speed records between the Wars, and Dylan Thomas's much-loved Laugharne. The tall cliffs, sands and cockle beds of the Gower Peninsula form another Area of Outstanding Natural Beauty. To the east is the breathtaking contrast between a long stretch of glimmering beach and the billowing smokestacks and flaming chimneys of Port Talbot's gargantuan steelworks.

Along the Bristol Channel shore, the industrial revolution transformed little Glamorgan fishing harbours and dozy coastal ports into teeming, blackened industrial antheaps. In 1914, 11 million tons of coal were shipped out from Barry and another 10 million tons from Cardiff. Today King Coal has been dethroned and his territory is being 'greened' and regenerated.

LLANDUDNO
Conwy

3 MILES (5 KM) NORTH OF CONWY

Llandudno and the White Rabbit

At the age of 80 Alice Liddell, the real-life heroine of *Alice in Wonderland* and *Through the Looking Glass*, remembered Lewis Carroll's visits to Llandudno during summer holidays when she was young, 'and our games on the sandhills together'. She was the daughter of Henry Liddell, Dean of Christ Church, Oxford and a colleague of Carroll, who was a friend of the family and adored the young Alice. So perhaps it was the rabbits on the Great Orme which inspired the immortal figure of the White Rabbit and Alice's adventures down the mysterious rabbit hole, as Llandudno likes to think.

A steamer has tied up at Llandudno's Victorian pier, one of the finest in the country

With sandy beaches fore and aft, and the two looming limestone headlands of the Great Orme and the Little Orme to port and starboard, Llandudno is delightfully situated. It was developed in the 1850s by the local landowners, the Mostyn family, and beautifully planned, with a 2-mile promenade along the sweetly curving North Shore and a grid of wide, tree-lined streets. The town has retained its Victorian character, dignity and charm, and has, incidentally, the best shopping in North Wales. Llandudno is consequently an entirely appropriate home for the Alice in Wonderland Centre, in the Rabbit Hole, with its displays on this quintessential Victorian fantasy. The original Alice was the daughter of the Liddell family of Oxford, who brought her here for summer holidays as a child. Their house was where the Gogarth Abbey Hotel stands now, on the West Shore, and a statue of the White Rabbit (the busy little character who was always afraid of being late) by F W Forrester was unveiled here in 1933 by David Lloyd George. The handsome Victorian pier extends 2296 feet (700m) out into the bay, and the town has all the expected seaside entertainments: boat trips, band concerts, theatre

The 1930s statue of the White Rabbit recalls the town's links with Alice in Wonderland

shows, discos, dancing, cabaret, sailing and fishing, riding and pony trekking. A large collection of dolls is at home to callers at Childhood Revisited, with toys, lace and fans, a model railway and a collection of motorcycles. Llandudno Museum covers the local history, and Oriel Mostyn is a lively art gallery. Copper was mined on the Great Orme in the Bronze Age and the mine has recently been opened to the public. In the 6th century St Tudno established his mission here. The town is named after him, as the *llan* or '11holy enclosure' of Tudno, and the little medieval church on the headland is dedicated to him. On the lower slopes of the Great Orme are semi-tropical gardens, and higher up is a country park. There are several ways to the 679 feet (207m) summit. One is the mile-long cable car ride, which is Britain's longest. Another is the electric tramway, which began operating in 1902 and until 1958 was powered by steam. A third is by road from the scenic Marine Drive, opened in 1878, which winds its way around the headland. Up at the top are a new interpretative centre and a nature trail, and from here there are wonderful views inland to the Snowdonian peaks and seawards to the Isle of Man.

Iron Tightrope

The Menai Bridge was Telford's characteristically bold and dramatic way of getting his new road across the strait to Anglesey. It had to be set high above the water to allow the biggest ships to sail under it, and it was to hang between two great towers on 16 giant iron chains. These were anchored to a massive cast-iron frame at each end, sunk deep into solid rock. The chains had to be floated out onto the strait on a raft and hoisted laboriously up into place. The first chain was tackled on 26 April 1825, watched by a huge throng of people on both banks and in boats. It took 1 1/2 hours to haul it up into position, when a tremendous cheer echoed from shore to shore and three of the Welsh workmen celebrated by running perilously across the chain high in the air to the other side. It was only 9 inches (23cm) wide.

One of the 'wonders of Wales': Thomas Telford's bridge strides across the Menai Strait

MENAI BRIDGE
Isle of Anglesey

2 MILES (3 KM) EAST OF LLANFAIR PG

*A*s its name suggests, this little Anglesey town owes its existence principally to the suspension bridge which the great engineer Thomas Telford designed to carry his London to Holyhead road in splendour over the powerful tides and swirling currents of the Menai Strait. The bridge opened to traffic in 1826, replacing the previous ferry, though it swung so violently in high winds that coachmen and passengers were sometimes too frightened to cross it. With a central span of 579 feet (177m), this was the largest suspension bridge in the world when it was completed, and one of the supreme engineering feats of the 19th century. There is a fine view of it from the promenade called Belgian Walk, which was built during World War I by refugees from Belgium. A causeway leads out into the strait to Church Island and the simple 15th-century church dedicated to St Tysilio, a wandering Christian missionary who built a humble church on this spot in the 7th century. The town also boasts an art gallery and a butterfly farm. A little to the west, the A5 road and the railway cross the strait on another bridge, originally designed by Robert Stephenson in 1850, and replaced after a serious fire in 1970.

*The cross is a monument to
St Dwyn, with the stumpy
1870s lighthouse behind*

LLANDDWYN ISLAND
Isle of Anglesey

3 MILES (5 KM) SOUTH-WEST OF NEWBOROUGH

Off the south-west coast of Anglesey, Llanddwyn Island is named after St Dwyn, or Dwynwen, a misty figure from far back in the Dark Ages of the 5th and 6th centuries. She was one of the many children of the legendary King Brychan, whose offspring numbered anything from 12 to 63 according to varying traditions. Dwyn was a devout Christian and determined to preserve her virginity, so when a suitor named Maelon wanted to marry her, she sadly rejected him and became a nun. At the same time she earnestly prayed to God that all true lovers should either achieve their desires or be freed of love's fever. She became the unofficial patron saint of lovers in Wales and her church at Llanddwyn attracted numerous pilgrims. Many came to consult the fishes in the saint's holy well, whose movements foretold the future. Today's visitors come for the vast expanse of sand and dunes, with breathtaking views of the Snowdonian mountains across the water. The island is part of the huge Newborough Warren nature reserve, with a great wealth of dune plants, as well as conifer forest and saltmarsh on the estuary of the River Cefni. St Dwyn's holy fishes have departed long since, but not far away, the delightful Anglesey Sea Zoo makes a most acceptable substitute.

SOUTH STACK
CLIFFS

The Chough

Named after its 'chough'-like call, this elegant member of the crow family is regularly seen at South Stack. Groups of four or five birds often wheel through the air, riding the updraughts off the cliffs and calling loudly. Choughs are easily recognised in flight by the long, red bill and finger-like wing tips. Their distinctive, high-pitched calls easily distinguish them from crows, ravens and jackdaws, which are also present here.

The cliffs at South Stack are particularly impressive

Dramatic cliff scenery, and easy access from Holyhead, make South Stack Cliffs a good place for walking – weather permitting – at any time of year. Those who come here for the wildlife, however, come in May and June, when the cliffs are thronged with nesting seabirds and the RSPB reserve's rich and varied flora is seen at its best. The reserve is at Anglesey's most westerly extremity, 3 miles (4.8km) west of Holyhead. The walk is about 2 miles (3.2km) long, and steep in places, with steps to climb. Follow signs from the town, and park in the first signposted car park.

❧❧❧❧

DIRECTIONS

1 From the car park follow the signs for the cliff path along an old stone wall. The walk leads through salt-pruned dwarf heath, with extensive patches of the diminutive spring squill and tormentil. Other plants in flower in late spring will include sea campion, thrift and the yellow-flowering field fleawort.

2 Take care as the path approaches the cliff, which is very sudden and precipitous. Immediately below you is a dramatic example of a sea-cliff stack, while to the left is Pen-las Rock where rock pipits – small brown birds – perch on rock ledges. The view south takes in less dramatic coastal scenery, while to the north is South Stack lighthouse and the dramatic cliffs.

3 Retrace your steps and then take the path north towards the lighthouse and cross the small wooden bridge over the culvert. Follow the coast path to the information centre at Ellin's Tower (which has well presented and up-to-date information on the wildlife and history of the area).

The maritime grassland in this area is worth a close look. There are cushions of the tiny sheepsbit scabious, wild carrot and kidney vetch, while on the sheer cliffs unusually large numbers of ox-eye daisies can be seen. Wall brown and silver-studded blue butterflies are common, and are particularly noticeable on either side of the newly turfed path. The buckshorn plaintain, a vigorous early coloniser, is there in abundance but will soon be replaced by plants of the sea-turf proper. To the left of the path grow plants typical of lime-rich grassland, while to the right swathes of heather, tormentil and bell heather show how a layer of peat changes the vegetation.

4 Leaving Ellin's Tower, walk up the slate steps to the cliff-edge. Puffins, razorbills, guillemots, fulmars and herring gulls can

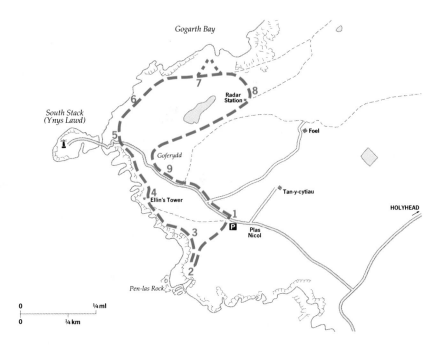

Gogarth Bay

South Stack
(Ynys Lawd)

Radar
Station

Foel

Goferydd

Ellin's Tower

Tan-y-cytiau

HOLYHEAD

Plas
Nicol

Pen-las Rock

0   ¼ ml

0   ¼ km

Grassland and Heath
The cliffs and their birdlife make up only a part of the natural history interest of the South Stack area. The sedimentary rock of the cliffs is overlain by both basic and acid soils, ensuring a variety of plant life that is remarkable for such an exposed coast. Swathes of sea campion and thrift are intermingled with extensive areas of heather and dwarf gorse. Rarities such as spotted rock-rose and field fleawort are easily seen in the areas of fine maritime grassland, where spring squill and English stonecrop are also found. The heathland shelters some extensive patches of heath spotted orchid. Super-ficially this orchid is similar to the common spotted orchid, but is almost always found growing on acid soils. Inhabitants of the heathlands include populations of both adder and common lizard and, rather surprisingly for such a well visited site, various nesting waders. Look out also for butterflies. Silver-studded blues may be seen among the dry grassland, while marsh fritillaries prefer the damper areas.

all be seen here. During the summer months this is a good area in which to watch for hunting peregrines. On the cliffs around you are swathes of spring squill, and a few patches of the rare spotted rock-rose. This flowers in June, but you will only see it in bloom if you visit before midday, when it sheds its petals.

5 Continue up the steep steps and then take the cliff path (rather than the road). This is the most difficult stretch of walking, but rewarding for the pale green lichen called sea ivory. Several other lichen species festoon the granite rocks on either side of the path. Also worth exploring is the good maritime grassland, where patches of the white-flowering scurvy-grass may be found in spring. Later in the spring, the yellow flowers of cat sear and hawkbit become more noticeable.

6 Cross the low wall and walk to the picnic tables which overlook the lighthouse of South Stack, then follow the path up the gentle slope to the old World War II look-out post. Two characteristic plants of the cliffs grow immediately in front of the building: the green, straggly sea beet, which has waxy leaves to reduce the effect of the salt-laden winds, and the more delicate scentless mayweed, which minimises its water loss by having very finely serrated leaves. Walk through the extensive areas of dwarf heather; within this are patches of heath spotted orchids, which particularly like the acid soil.

7 Follow the path around the wet hollow or pool, but you can leave the path for a short detour to look over Gogarth Bay where grey seals often haul out.

8 Walk back to the path and pass the radar station to reach the opposite side of the pool. The wet area is important for butterflies such as the marsh fritillary, a small, brightly coloured, chequered orange and fawn butterfly whose caterpillars feed on the devilsbit scabious leaves found in such areas.

9 Continue through the heathland back to the road, and follow it back to the car park. As you go, watch for whitethroats on the telegraph wires.

❀

AN ABUNDANCE OF BIRD LIFE
Birdwatchers are unlikely to leave South Stack disappointed. The area is good for passage birds, including the occasional rarity, in both spring and autumn. It is always worth keeping an eye out to sea for gannets and Manx shearwaters; and in the breeding season three of Britain's species of auk – puffins, guillemots and razorbills – may be more easily seen flying and fishing off shore, rather than on the inaccessible cliff ledges. Guillemots are by far the most numerous, and can easily be distinguished from razorbills by their more slender, pointed bills. Both species are more agile in the water than in the air or on land.

Better views of the nesting seabirds can be obtained in the information centre, Ellin's Tower, where a remote-control camera beams close-up pictures to a television. It is not unusual to have the opportunity to watch peregrines hunting rock doves and other birds – an unforgettable experience. Choughs, distinctive members of the crow family which were once much more common, are also resident on the reserve.

A rainbow curves above Aberdaron, on a spectacular stretch of the Welsh coast

ABERDARON
Gwynedd

13 MILES (21KM) SOUTH-WEST OF NEFYN

Close to 'the Land's End of Wales', the old fishing village at the mouth of the River Daron was a staging point on the medieval pilgrimage to Bardsey Island, which lies off the tip of the Lleyn (rhymes with 'clean') Peninsula. A 14th-century rest house for pilgrims is now a café and gift shop, and with its simple stone cottages, sandy beach, sea fishing and boat trips, the village is an engaging holiday resort. At high tide the waves roll up against the sea wall of the 12th-century church. To the south-west, the peninsula ends in the savage cliffs of Braich y Pwyll (National Trust), looking across a turbulent 2 mile (3km) stretch of water to Bardsey Island. Pilgrims took a refreshing draught from St Mary's Well and prayed for a safe crossing at the now ruined chapel, before entrusting themselves to the tidal races and whirlpools that gave the island its Welsh name of Ynys Enlli, 'isle of currents'. The Celts had a deep religious feeling for remote islands in the west and a monastery was built on Bardsey in the Dark Ages. So many pilgrims left their bones here that it became known as 'the island of 20,000 saints'. According to local tradition Merlin, the master magician of the Arthurian legends, retired to the House of Glass on Bardsey and has never been seen since. Now owned by a private trust, the island houses a bird and field observatory.

Tranquillity of a calm evening by the quay at Abersoch

ABERSOCH
Gwynedd

7 MILES (11 KM) SOUTH-WEST OF PWLLHELI

With sandy beaches and a picturesque harbour, Abersoch is a popular sailing and holiday resort. It becomes quite crowded in summer, when the water of the bay is dotted with white sails. There are boat trips to Bardsey Island and to St Tudwal's Islands, a pair of small offshore islands which in 1934 were bought by Clough Williams-Ellis, the creator of Portmeirion, to preserve them from development. The ruins of a small medieval priory stand on the more northerly one. St Tudwal was a 6th-century Welsh missionary who emigrated to Brittany and founded a monastery there. The Lleyn area, 'the little Wales beyond Wales', was still described in the 1930s as a remote wilderness whose inhabitants lived in happy isolation from the modern world. The motor car and the tourist industry have put an end to that, but the Lleyn is still a stronghold of the Welsh language and traditional Welsh ways, with a certain remoteness about it. To the west of Abersoch, the remarkable 15th-century church of Llanengan has two of everything – two naves, two altars, two rood screens – and halfway between Abersoch and Aberdaron, the lovely old manor house of Plas yn Rhiw (National Trust) looks south over Cardigan Bay.

PORTMEIRION
Gwynedd

2 MILES (3 KM) SOUTH-WEST OF PENRHYNDEUDRAETH

My dear dog gone before
To that unknown and silent
*   shore*
Shall we not meet as
*   heretofore*
Some summer morning?'
Epitaph in the dogs' cemetery
at Portmeirion

Portmeirion is unique. It is a village with no inhabitants. It is completely artificial, has no history and is the inspired creation of one man. It is also one of the most magical places on earth, a vision of towers and domes, courtyards and arches, multi-coloured houses, statues and fountains, stairways and shops, grottos and cool colonnades. It is promenaded by peacocks, and at every turning there are fresh, intriguing grey-domed Pantheon, added in 1959 to correct 'a severe dome deficiency', has part of an ornate 19th-century fireplace as a grand façade. The Town Hall contains a 17th-century ballroom from a demolished Flintshire mansion. An 18th-century colonnade from a house near Bristol dignifies the central piazza; some of the apparently substantial buildings are merely façades. The house on the site was converted into a hotel and entertained

The house called Chantry was intended to be a studio for Augustus John; the onion dome conceals a boiler chimney

perspectives. Portmeirion's creator, Clough Williams-Ellis, cut his teeth as an architect in the Garden City movement. In 1925 he bought a 19th-century house and a tangled, overgrown area of land on the north bank of the sandy estuary of the Glaslyn and the Dwyryd, which had been owned for years by an eccentric recluse. He set about bringing to life a fantasy Mediterranean village on the cliffside, which occupied him for more than 50 years. Many of the buildings, or parts of them, were rescued from the scrap heap, and he liked to call Portmeirion his 'home for fallen buildings'. The tall campanile contains stones from a 12th-century castle. The rafts of celebrities, including Noël Coward, who wrote *Blithe Spirit* here in 1941. Badly damaged by a fire in 1981, it was sumptuously restored and reopened in 1988. It stands on the water's edge, and 'tied up' at the quay is a Williams-Ellis joke – a stone boat. Portmeirion was the setting for the 1960s TV classic 'The Prisoner' and its devotees still make reverent pilgrimages here. The village stands in more than 70 acres of woodlands, and there is even a cemetery for the estate's dogs, started around 1900 by the eccentric old lady from whom Sir Clough bought the estate. It is a touching place, and the tradition of burying much-loved pets there has been continued.

Looking up the steep hillside to the Pantheon – the elaborate front is part of a 19th-century fireplace

ABERYSTWYTH
Ceredigion

34 MILES (55 KM) NORTH-EAST OF CARDIGAN

The entrance to the sedate cliff railway, which opened in 1896

A holiday resort and the principal shopping town and 'capital' of the Cardigan Bay area, Aberystwyth – or Aber for short – has taken a leading part in modern Welsh patriotism. The Welsh Language Society has its base here, Wales's first university opened here in the 1870s and the town is home to the august National Library of Wales, whose unrivalled collection of books and material relating to Wales and the Celtic countries contains venerable manuscripts of early Welsh poetry and laws. Aberystwyth's seafront promenade runs along the gracefully curving shore, backed by Victorian terraces. The university's original building began life as a Victorian Gothic grand hotel, after the arrival of the railway in 1864 had put the town on the map for visitors. The ruins of a 13th-century castle stand on the headland to the south, with the yacht harbour beyond. Britain's longest electric cliff railway, opened in 1896, runs very slowly and gently up a 2-in-1 gradient to the 430 feet (131m) high summit of Constitution Hill. At the top there is a Camera Obscura, whose all-seeing eye gazes hawk-like over 1000 square miles (2590sq km) of spectacular scenery. The plush Edwardian music hall, formerly the Coliseum, has been restored as the Ceredigion Museum (retaining its stage and balconies), with an excellent folk collection including a reconstructed cottage. The cheerful Vale of Rheidol Railway steams its scenic way inland from Aberystwyth to the beauty spot of Devil's Bridge.

FISHGUARD
Pembrokeshire

9 MILES (14 KM) NORTH-EAST OF ST DAVID'S

*I*n the 1971 film of *Under Milk Wood*, the picturesque oldest part of Fishguard – the Lower Town down by the harbour – did duty for Dylan Thomas's fictional seaport of Llareggub. It has appeared in other films, too, including *Moby Dick*. The photogenic town's real, Welsh name is Abergwaun and it stands where the River Gwaun flows out to sea. A fishing harbour and coastal port in its time, it was a centre for trade with Ireland and Chester, and late in the 18th century some 50 coastal cargo boats plied from here, exporting oats and salted herring. Today the beautiful harbour shelters small sailing craft and the yachting fraternity. The Royal Oak has mementos of the last invasion of Britain, a comical episode when a small army of French drunks landed here in 1797, and St Mary's Church has the grave of the redoubtable local heroine Jemima Nicholas. A woman of formidable physique and alarming aspect, she led the local resistance, capturing no fewer than 14 of the enemy single-handed, wielding only a pitchfork. You can buy traditional Welsh laver bread (made from seaweed) in Fishguard, or you can catch the ferry for the short crossing to Rosslare in Ireland from the harbour at Goodwick, where a 2,000ft (610m) breakwater was constructed before World War I to create a deep-water harbour, in the vain hope of attracting the cross-Atlantic liners.

French With Tears
The great day in Fishguard's history was 22 February 1797, during the French wars, when three enemy ships landed a rabble of some 1400 soldiers and ex-convicts near Carreg Wastad Point, under an American commander. They were meant to march on Chester and Liverpool, but in fact took the opportunity to get thoroughly drunk. The local people reacted vigorously and the story has it that the bemused invaders mistook the traditional red cloaks of the Welsh womenfolk for the scarlet uniforms of British infantry. They surrendered on 24 February and articles of peace were signed in the Royal Oak inn.

Rusting at low tide: Fishguard was once a busy coastal cargo port

THE
HEART OF WALES

Bwlch Nant-yr-Arian Forest Visitor Centre

The centre is located a little further along the A44 from Llywernog. Perched on the edge of a steep slope, it enjoys breathtaking views down the valley towards Aberystwyth. A well-laid out exhibition area introduces visitors to local history and the landscape, while the surrounding forests contain waymarked walks and picnic sites.

Rolling green hills near Aberystwyth

This pleasant 42-mile (68km) drive through the heart of Wales starts in Aberystwyth, the town which occupies the middle ground along Cardigan Bay, that great north to south arc of the Welsh coast. Inland, green farming country rises to the high plateaux and peaks of Plynlimon, a mountain range in the centre of Wales clothed in empty moorland and coniferous forest.

➤➤➤➤

DIRECTIONS

Leave Aberystwyth on the Pen-Glais road (sp. Machynlleth, A487) and, after passing the University campus on the right, turn left on to the B4572 (sp. Llangorwen, Clarach). In 1 mile follow the road round the hairpin bend and keep straight on through Llangorwen. Follow the road for about 3½ miles and, in Borth, turn left on to B4353 and continue through the town. Stay on the B4353, bear right at the edge of Ynyslas. In ¾

mile cross the Afon Leri, then the railway and the reclaimed marshland, bear left in Llancynfelyn to Tre'r-ddôl. Turn right on to the A487 (sp. Aberystwyth) and pass through Tre Taliesin to reach Talybont. At the White Lion turn left, unclassified, then left again and follow the signs to Nant-y-Moch. Soon after bear right, 200 yards on bear left on to a single track road and gradually ascend the side of Cwm Ceulan. At the summit bear right, pass through a forested area, go alongside Nant-y-Moch Reservoir. Cross the top of the dam, climb to 1,300ft then pass the Dinas Reservoir before reaching Ponterwyd. Turn right on to the A44 Aberystwyth road, pass Llywernog Silver-Lead Mine and after a further mile on the A44 pass the Bwlch Nant-yr-Arian Forest Visitor Centre. Continue on the A44 and make a long, winding descent down the Melindwr Valley. Pass through Goginan, Capel Bangor and Llanbadarn Fawr before re-entering Aberystwyth.

>>ON THE TOUR >>

Aberystwyth

This dignified seaside resort is also a university town, and a shopping centre for the villages scattered between the mountains and the sea. Once known as the fashionable 'Biarritz of Wales', Aberystwyth preserves its Victorian character most convincingly. The view along the promenade, a curving seafront lined with pastel-shaded, bay-windowed hotels and guest houses, has changed little over the years.

The seafront ends at Constitution Hill, which can be climbed on foot or more appropriately by the Cliff Railway – 'a conveyance of gentle folk since 1896' and the only one of its kind in Wales. The hill's summit has another attraction redolent of the Victorian Age – a Camera Obscura, whose all-seeing lens scans Cardigan Bay and over 25 mountain peaks. Aberystwyth's 'museum within a music hall' is another convincing period piece.

The headland at the southern end of the promenade close to the harbour is occupied by the ruins of Aberystwyth Castle. The fortress, begun in 1277, was one of Edward I's first castles in Wales. In 1404 it was captured by the Welsh leader Owain Glyndwr, though it suffered its greatest damage during the Civil War.

A large university campus is spread out across the hillside above the town. It is the home of the National Library of Wales, whose collection of over 2 million books includes some of the oldest manuscripts in the Welsh language.

Aberystwyth Station is the starting point of the narrow-gauge Vale of Rheidol Railway, which runs for 12 miles (19km) to a mountain terminus at Devil's Bridge.

Borth

Borth is a straggling seaside centre on a flat coastal plain, with a huge three-mile sandy beach. It consists mainly of caravan parks located close to a long main street.

Nant-y-Moch Reservoir

The mountain road from the square of Talybont climbs up into the wastes of Plynlimon. Here, below the mountain range's 2,468ft (752m) summit, a huge man-made lake of over 7,000 million gallons has been created. Unlike the other lakes in Mid Wales, Nant-y-Moch's inky black waters are not used for consumption, but as a source of power. The lake plays a central role in the Rheidol Hydroelectric Power Scheme. The road runs across the top of a 172-ft (52m) high dam before following the River Rheidol southwards to the smaller Dinas reservoir, also part of the hydro-electric scheme.

Llywernog Silver-Lead Mine

The A44 westwards past Ponterwyd runs through peaceful countryside in which it is difficult to imagine that any form of industrial activity once took place. Yet in the 17th to 19th centuries, the minerals of Mid Wales were mined extensively. The overgrown spoil heaps at Llywernog are evidence of mining activity dating from the 1740s. Llywernog's mine closed in the 1880s, lying derelict until its restoration and re-opening as an open-air museum some 100 years later. The 7-acre site contains old buildings, water-wheels, a 'Miner's Trail', prospecting tunnel, exhibition and an audio-visual display. Closed November to mid-March.

Llanbadarn Fawr

This village, now a suburb of Aberystwyth, reveals its historic and religious significance through the size of its church. The unexpected grandeur of the church reflects the influential role which Llanbadarn Fawr once played in Welsh affairs. A religious community founded here in the 6th century became a celebrated centre of scholarship. The present church, which is one of the largest in Wales, dates from around 1200.

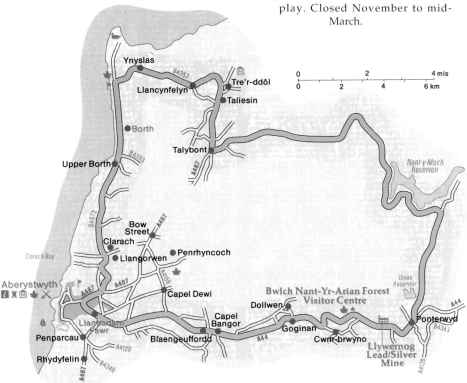

From the lifeboat station there are boat trips to Ramsey Island, seen in the distance

ST DAVID'S
Pembrokeshire

15 MILES (24 KM) WEST OF CARMARTHEN

*I*n the 19th century, when Sir George Gilbert Scott was restoring St David's Cathedral, human bones were found hidden in a recess behind the high altar. They were the remains of two people, and perhaps three, and the probability is that these were the bones of St David himself and two other local saints, secreted away at the Reformation. Certainly the existence today of Britain's smallest city – really no more than a village – bears witness to the lasting influence of Wales's favourite saint, who founded a monastery here in the 6th century, and whose feast day on 1 March has become a rallying day for Welsh patriotic feeling. Celtic Christianity communicated by sea and this remote part of the Welsh coast was then a hub of missionary travel between Ireland, Wales, the south-west of England and Brittany. David (Dewi in Welsh) is the only Welsh saint to have been canonised by the Roman Catholic Church, and in 1120 Pope Calixtus II ruled that two pilgrimages to distant St David's

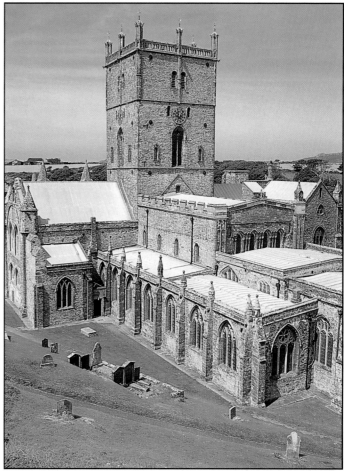

The largest church in Wales is tucked away out of sight in a dip of land

should count as equal to one pilgrimage to Rome. Pilgrims did indeed flock to the spot and it was their offerings which paid for the cathedral, Wales's largest church, which is tucked away in a dip by the little River Alun. It dates from all periods since the 12th century, and a striking feature of the Norman nave is its pronounced slope, with a rise of 14 feet (4m) from the west end to the high altar. The impressive bishop's throne of about 1500 stands almost 30 feet (10m) high, and in front of the high altar is the tomb of Edmund Tudor, father of Henry VII. Across the stream is the ruined Bishops Palace (Cadw). Bishop Barlow in the 16th century found himself with five daughters who needed dowries, so he gradually stripped the lead off the roof and sold it. (Suitably provided

for, they all five went on to marry bishops.) Other pleasures of a visit to this historic and tranquil place include not one but two aquariums – the Marine Life Centre and the Oceanarium – the rare breed animals at the Farm Park, and the bygones in the Lleithyr Farm Museum. There are boat trips to Ramsey Island from the St Justinian lifeboat station and attractive walks along the cliffs. This area is part of the Pembrokeshire Coast National Park, which was set aside to protect some of the most spectacularly impressive and beautiful coastal scenery in Britain. With a wealth of birdlife and plants, there are also remains of centuries of human activity, including kilns, quays and warehouses left behind from the busy coastal traffic of the days before World War I.

In the Steps of St David

According to pious legend, St David's mother, St Non, gave birth to him on the cliffs above St Non's Bay during a wild storm, and as a sign of the child's special sanctity a spring welled up between her feet – the same one which rises near her ruined chapel today. David grew up to be an inspiring Christian leader and an austere teetotaller and vegetarian. He drank no beer or wine, only water, and his fondness for leeks is said to have made them the Welsh national emblem.

The marina and the lightship keep the watch where Viking war galleys used to sleep

MILFORD HAVEN
Pembrokeshire

9 MILES (15 KM) WEST OF PEMBROKE

The Western Cleddau, the Eastern Cleddau and several lesser streams combine to form the huge natural harbour of Milford Haven. Viking fleets wintered here and medieval English expeditions mustered here to invade Ireland. The entrance is guarded by the Dale and Angle peninsulas (both names are Norse), reinforced in the 19th century by a bristling array of forts. The Dale Peninsula is both the sunniest place in Wales and the windiest, but the sheltered waters in the haven have made Dale itself a busy sailing and watersports centre. Near by is the spot in Mill Bay where Henry Tudor landed in 1485 on his way to win the throne of England. The town of Milford Haven was laid out as a planned dockyard town some 200 years ago, and the first inhabitants, astonishingly enough, were Quaker whalermen and their families who immigrated here from Nantucket. Their meeting house dates from 1811. The fascinating story of the town is told in the Heritage and Maritime Museum, and the Haven Lightship is open to visitors. It was not until the 1960s that Milford Haven developed as a port for giant oil tankers and acquired its futuristic landscape of oil refineries and chemical installations.

❖

PEMBROKE
Pembrokeshire

29 MILES (47 KM) SOUTH-EAST OF CARMARTHEN

❖

*The boats have peaceful
intentions, but the castle
seems to be cocking a wary
eye at them all the same*

A grim and enduring symbol of the domination of South Wales by Norman warlords, the mighty battlements and towers of Pembroke Castle rear up above the town, the enormous circular keep standing 75 feet (22m) high, with walls 16 feet (5m) thick. The castle was built during the 13th century by the famous knight William Marshal – a peerless jouster, he made a fortune fighting in tournaments – and his five stalwart sons. In 1452 the stronghold came to Jasper Tudor, whose nephew Harri, the future King Henry VII, was born here and probably grew up within these walls. During the Civil War the castle was attacked by each side in turn. In 1648 Oliver Cromwell came in person to superintend a siege which lasted for seven weeks of incessant artillery bombardment until the garrison surrendered. Substantial stretches of the town's medieval walls have survived. Below the castle, the Museum of the Home has a fascinating collection of items of domestic life over the last 300 years, ranging from fashion accessories and smoking paraphernalia by way of love tokens, games and lamps, to sewing gear and kitchen bygones. To the north-west, Pembroke Dock was once an important naval base and shipyard.

A Fortified Coastline

The sea is a barrier, but it is also a bridge, and at strategic points around Britain's coastline the remains of formidable defences testify to centuries of determined resistance to invaders and marauders. Already, in prehistoric times, natural strongpoints like Flamborough Head were fortified with earthworks, and in Scotland refuge towers or brochs were built, like the two close to Brora on the north-east coast.

Caernarfon Castle, Edward I's symbol of his imperial might in Wales was sited to be supplied by sea in times of siege

In the 3rd century AD, when Saxon raiders were plundering the southern coasts, the Roman authorities built the forts of the Saxon Shore, a chain of strongholds from the Solent to the Wash. Defended by massive walls and catapult artillery, they include Portchester, Pevensey and Richborough. The Normans took over some of these fortresses and constructed others of their own.

In Wales the conquering Edward I built coastal castles which could be kept supplied from the sea: Beaumaris, Conwy, Caernarfon, Harlech. Along the Scottish coastline rise louring keeps where local warlords controlled the sea approaches and defied land armies: rose-red Tantallon, the impregnable Douglas stronghold on the Lothian coast; the black Campbell hold of Dunstaffnage on its crag above the Firth of Lorne; and grim and sea-girt Kiessimul, where MacNeill of Barra docked his chiefly war-galley.

England's southern shore was the most vulnerable to attack from the Continent, and the Tudors built new, state-of-the-art fortresses for defence against naval artillery. Pendennis Castle at Falmouth guards the entrance to Carrick Roads, Southsea Castle protects the approach to Portsmouth Harbour, Walmer and Deal Castles mind the flat, exposed Kentish shore. Three centuries later, to meet the threat of Napoleon's invasion barges, the Martello towers were built along the south-eastern coast of England – fortified gun

platforms sited so that each overlapped the field of fire of its neighbours.

In the 1860s, when French invasion was feared again, formidable defences were thrown up, including the extraordinary man-made armoured islands in Spithead. Immense, labyrinthine strongholds were dug deep into cliffs, like Fort Widley at Portsmouth and Fort Luton at Chatham. During the two world wars, fortresses like these were put into commission again, and even an old war-horse like Pevensey Castle, originally a Saxon Shore fort, was equipped with pillboxes against Hitler in 1940. At Dover, dominating the shortest passage across the Channel, there are defences of every period – from Roman days to the Hellfire Corner tunnels of World War II. The message from every period is the same: 'They shall not pass.'

Dover Castle: since Roman times massive fortifications have guarded the shortest crossing from France

132

A Host of Golden Daffodils
Tenby used to be known for its own special brand of wild daffodils, whose trumpets pointed upwards. They flowered early and were admired for their particularly vibrant colour. Demand for them was so strong that in the 1880s and 1890s half a million bulbs were sent up to London every year, and the plant came close to extinction. They used to grow in great profusion on Giltar Point, south of the town.

In Praise of Tenby
'You may travel the world over, but you will find nothing more beautiful: it is so restful, so colourful and so unspoilt.'
Augustus John

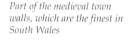

Part of the medieval town walls, which are the finest in South Wales

TENBY
Pembrokeshire

9 MILES (14 KM) EAST OF PEMBROKE

People have been singing Tenby's praises enthusiastically since the 9th century, when an anonymous Welsh poet composed verses in honour of the fine fortress on the bright headland and the courage and generosity of its late lord, a chieftain named Bleiddudd. More recent eulogies focus on the beauty of the old harbour lying in the headland's shelter, the handsome Regency houses overlooking it and the charm of medieval Tenby, with its narrow streets hemmed in by town walls which are the best preserved in South Wales. The famous Five Arches form the barbican to the old south gate. The walls were built in the 13th century and later strengthened, but were still

not adequate to withstand Parliamentary artillery in the siege of 1644, when the town quickly surrendered. Tenby was a prosperous fishing and cargo port, and at one time a smuggling haven for brandy brought across from France. The castle ruins on the headland today are not those of Bleiddudd's fortress, but of the later, medieval castle, built after Norman barons had conquered this part of Wales. The museum here covers the local history, and there is a good collection of pictures by Welsh artists, including Augustus John and his sister Gwen, who grew up here (he was born in Tenby in 1878). Also born in Tenby, in 1510, was Robert Recorde, the mathematician who invented the

Small boats nestle in Tenby's sheltered harbour, below Castle Hill

sign = for 'equals'. There is a memorial to him in St Mary's, claimed to be the largest parish church in Wales and a mark of Tenby's medieval prosperity. Another is the Tudor Merchant's House (National Trust), the home of a well-to-do businessman of about 1500, and probably the oldest house in the town. Early in the 19th century Sir William Paxton, a wealthy banker, took Tenby in hand and began to convert it into a seaside resort of charm and character which attracted many Victorian visitors. He built Laston House for the indoor seawater swimming baths, with a Greek inscription on the building meaning, 'The sea washes away all mankind's ills.' Today, besides sandy beaches for washing away the ills, Tenby offers its visitors fishing, watersports, golf and an aquarium. There are boat trips to Caldey Island, where the Cistercian monastery is open to male visitors only, and the monks make perfumes from the island's wildflowers.

SWANSEA
Swansea

35 MILES (56 KM) WEST OF CARDIFF

Growing Up in Swansea

'I was born in a large Welsh industrial town at the beginning of the Great War: an ugly, lovely town (or so it was, and is, to me), crawling, sprawling, slummed, unplanned, jerry-villa'd and smug-suburbed by the side of a long and splendid-curving shore where truant boys and sandfield boys and old anonymous men, in the tatters and hangovers of a hundred charity suits, beachcombed, idled and paddled, threw stones into the sea for the barking, outcast dogs, and on Saturday summer afternoons listened to the militant music of salvation and hell-fire preached from a soap-box.'
Dylan Thomas, broadcast talk (1943)

Sunrise over the docks at Swansea

It used to be said that the only good thing from Swansea was the road out, but Dylan Thomas's 'ugly, lovely town' – he was born here in 1914, at 5 Cwmdonkin Drive and played in Cwmdonkin Park – has begun to recover in style from its painful post-war collapse as a premier industrial port. The new Maritime Quarter, created in the 1980s, has brought the old South Dock, off the River Tawe (the city's Welsh name is Abertawe), back to life as a marina. The quarter is equipped with lively new architecture that is positively pleasurable to look at, a big leisure centre, a theatre and pleasant places to eat and drink. The Maritime and Industrial Museum has a working woollen mill inside, historic vessels to explore on the dock alongside, and lots of industrial machinery and transport exhibits. A short way inland is the splendid covered market, in a modern building but wholeheartedly traditional in spirit, and purveying Welsh lamb, seaweed laver bread and local cockles in ample quantities. Dignified Swansea Museum was the first in Wales, and the Glynn Vivian Art Gallery has delightful Swansea and Nantgarw porcelain to add to its pictures and sculptures. There are sandy beaches along the shore and all the scenic beauty of the Gower Peninsula in easy reach.

CARDIFF
Cardiff

21 MILES (34 KM) SOUTH-EAST OF MERTHYR TYDFIL

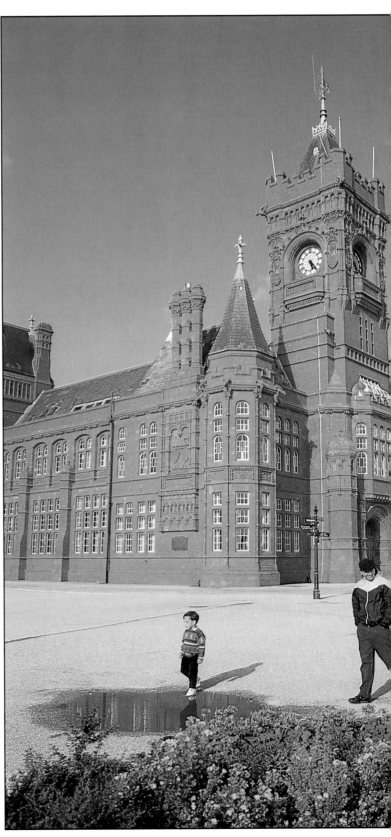

*I*n less than 200 years Cardiff has changed radically – twice. An inconspicuous port with a population of 1000 in 1801, the industrial revolution transformed it into one of the world's greatest coal ports, as the pits in the valleys to the north poured 'black diamonds' into it like water into a funnel. Then oil replaced coal, and since the 1950s Cardiff has turned itself into a civilised and engaging capital city for Wales. The docks area is now being massively regenerated. The leading role in the 19th-century development was taken by the principal local landowners, the Marquesses of Bute, whose most striking memorial is Cardiff Castle. This wonderful, wildly over-the-top fantasy in honour of Christian chivalry and the Middle Ages was the creation of the 3rd Marquess and his brilliant architect, William Burges, who also built the Prisoner-of-Zenda dream fortress of Castell Coch on the northern outskirts. Products of the 20th century include the noble Civic Centre, the National Museum of Wales and the delightful Welsh Folk Museum at St Fagans. Welsh National Opera has its headquarters in Cardiff, and St David's Hall is a temple of music, as Cardiff Arms Park is of rugby. Excellent shopping, Victorian arcades and beautiful parks help to make this one of Britain's most enjoyable cities.

The magnificent Pierhead Building, part of Cardiff's restored maritime area

A section of the craggy Berwickshire coast

$\mathscr{S}$COTLAND

—◆—

*F*ew places in Scotland are more than 40 miles (64km) away from salt water. With a long, deeply indented coastline and hundreds of islands – 787 in all, according to an authoritative count – Scotland's history and character have been influenced strategically and economically by the presence of the sea. The original Scots were the seaborne Irish invaders of Argyll in the 6th century, and in the 9th they united with the Picts of the east. Meanwhile the Vikings were raiding and settling the north and west of Scotland. The Western Isles remained under Norse rule until the 13th century, and Orkney and Shetland until the 15th century.

All round the coast people naturally depended on fishing for food and there was smuggling to the west coast from Ireland (the contraband included salt), and to eastern harbours from Holland and Scandinavia. Aberdeen and Peterhead developed whaling fleets, and in Victorian times herring fishing became a major Scottish industry – at least until the 'silver darlings' were overfished.

At Scotland's extreme south-west tip the stark cliffs of the Mull of Galloway rear up above the maelstrom of the tides. This area may be far off today's beaten track, but for centuries, until the railway came, its harbours offered the swiftest routes to Ireland, north-west England and north Wales. Further north, sandy beaches and famous golf courses line the Ayrshire coast, with the islands of Arran and Bute positioned like inner and outer watchdogs to the Firth of Clyde and Scotland's 'other capital', Glasgow.

North again lies the entrancing coast of the western Highlands, where glimmering sea lochs reach far inland among the mountains and the sun goes down in splendour among the Isles, a country steeped in the magic of a romantic, often blood-drenched past. A procession of nostalgic and beautiful names, echoing with a tangled history of escapes and clearances – Lorne, Ardnamurchan, Moidart, Knoydart – leads to the island of Skye.

Further north still are the spectacular mountains and lochs of Wester Ross and the far Sutherland shore, leading on up to Cape Wrath. The dangerous waters of the Pentland Firth smash against the northern cliffs to Duncansby Head, where the coastline turns south down the eastern shore of Caithness. Scotland's eastern coast is less indented and dramatic than the western one, but the Dornoch Firth, the Moray Firth, the Firth of Tay and the Firth of Forth in succession bite deep into the land. Along the coast of Fife former fishing ports do duty as holiday and retirement centres until the Lothian shore runs down to Berwick and the Border.

PORTPATRICK
Dumfries and Galloway

6 MILES (10 KM) SOUTH OF STRANRAER

What Gretna Green was to runaway English couples, so was Portpatrick to eloping lovers from Ireland – a place where they could be married with no inconvenient questions asked. Until 1826 the Church of Scotland ran a profitable trade in quick and easy weddings here: 'landed on Saturday, called on Sunday, married on Monday', as the saying went. The Rhinns Peninsula at Scotland's south-west corner is the closest point to Ireland, and Portpatrick was the Scottish end of the 21-mile passage to Donaghadee in Ulster. The mails to Ireland took this route, while Irish cattle in bellowing thousands came the

other way. The snag was that Portpatrick's harbour lay at the mercy of the savage south-westerly gales. A pier was built in the 1770s, but it was not adequate and new harbour works on a massive scale began in 1820. The sea swept them all contemptuously away, and in 1849 the packet boats carrying mail, cargo and passengers to Ireland were transferred to nearby Stranraer. Portpatrick was left to develop as a pleasant small resort for sailing, sea-fishing, and nowadays watersports. The 17th-century church has an unusual Irish-style round tower, and the graveyard is the final resting place of many who died in shipwrecks on this harsh coast.

Portpatrick and its rocky harbour, seen from the southern cliffs

AYR
South Ayrshire

✤

12 MILES (19 KM) SOUTH-WEST OF KILMARNOCK

✤

'Auld Ayr, wham ne'er a toun surpasses
For honest men and bonnie lasses.'
Robert Burns, *Tam o' Shanter* (1791)

The Burns Monument with its formal gardens, and the single-arched Brig o' Doon

The principal seaside resort on this stretch of coast – its broad, sandy beach is said to be the most heavily trodden in Scotland – Ayr has a past going far back beyond William Wallace's burning alive of English soldiers in their wooden barracks here in 1297. In medieval days, the town was Scotland's leading west coast harbour. By the 18th century it was trading across the Atlantic, and in the 19th it became a major industrial port. At the same time, as sea-bathing became fashionable, Ayr blossomed as a smart resort for the local gentry, whose town residences have been transformed into hotels and boarding houses. The attractive parks are a legacy of this period and, as the names of Troon and Turnberry suggest, this is prime golfing territory. Many visitors to Ayr are pilgrims on the trail of the poet Robert Burns. He was baptised in the 17th-century Auld Kirk, and he and his friends used to meet in an alehouse which is now the Tam o' Shanter Museum. The cottage where he was born in 1759 is on the southern outskirts of the town, with a museum of his manuscripts and personal belongings. Thomas Hamilton designed the nearby Burns Monument in graceful classical style in 1820.

Lighting the Shore

The lighthouse-keepers of the popular stereotype, cooped up for weeks at a time in lonely sea-towers, are figures of the past. Today's lighthouses need no human attendants to operate the lights that are so vital to safety at sea.

Britain's oldest lighthouse is the ruined Roman one on the cliff at Dover. A fire burned in a brazier on top, fanned by the draught up the tower, to aid ships entering Dover harbour. In the Middle Ages beacon lights were maintained here and there along the coast by monks and anchorites. A hermit named Richard Reedbarrow kept a fire burning to warn ships at Spurn Head at the mouth of the Humber, where a long succession of beacons and lighthouses have been eroded away by the sea. On the Dorset coast, the chapel on St Aldhelm's Head, near Worth

Matravers, apparently doubled as a lighthouse, and the Benedictines of Abbotsbury kept a fire burning in St Catherine's Chapel.

Coastal lights and signals were not always evidence of humanitarian principles. According to tradition, the Abbot of Aberbrothock installed a bell on the dangerous Inchcape Reef, offshore from Arbroath on Scotland's east coast, to lure ships to their doom and his profit. When the first lighthouses were proposed for Cornwall, there was determined opposition from the local people, who feared that these newfangled

Looking out over a deceptively placid sea from the Nash Point lighthouse on the Glamorgan coast

installations would reduce the number of wrecks they were accustomed to plunder.

In the 1690s a ship-owner named Henry Winstanley built a fantastical-looking lighthouse on the savage Eddystone rocks in the English Channel, which took a regular toll of ships approaching Plymouth. He and his lighthouse were swept away by a vengeful storm in 1703. A second, wooden lighthouse burned down in 1735 and was replaced by a simple stone tower, designed by John Smeaton, which became the model for all subsequent tower lighthouses. The upper part of it now stands on Plymouth Hoe.

In England and Wales the Brotherhood of Trinity House, founded by Henry VIII, was ultimately given the responsibility for constructing and maintaining lighthouses. In Scotland this duty fell to the Commissioners of Northern Lights, and a period of intense activity around the turn of the 18th and 19th centuries was dominated by the remarkable Stevenson dynasty. The great Robert Stevenson (grandfather of the writer Robert Louis Stevenson) planted the Bell Rock lighthouse on the Inchcape Reef. His son Alan built the 200ft (60m) tower on the Muckle Flugga Rock in Shetland, still the northernmost lighthouse in Britain.

The graceful tower lighthouse on St Mary's Island, north of Whitley Bay on the Tyne and Wear coast

*Looking over Inveraray's
white-harled houses to
Loch Fyne*

INVERARAY
Argyll and Bute

19 MILES (31 KM) NORTH-EAST OF LOCHGILPHEAD

Clan Campbell's capital stands on the west bank of Loch Fyne, deep among the mountain fastnesses of Argyll. The original settlement of heather-thatched cottages huddled in the protective shadow of the castle, the stronghold of the Campbell chiefs, who became Dukes of Argyll. In 1743 the 3rd Duke resolved to build a brand-new castle and a brand-new town, rather further away, and these were built over the next 70 years and more. The principal planners and architects were Roger Morris, William Adam (father of the more famous Robert) and Robert Mylne, and the work was nobly conceived and executed. Inveraray Castle itself is a turreted Gothicky pile. Its superb interiors by Mylne were restored after a severe fire in 1975. In the town, the inn and the gaol (now open as a tourist attraction) were among the first of the new buildings, along with the pier for the fishing boats. The town's kindly motto was 'May you always have a catch of herring', but the Loch Fyne fishery is a thing of the past. The town's dignified main street runs from the old market cross past Mylne's parish church, which was divided in two by a wall inside, to separate the services in Gaelic from those in English.

PLOCKTON
Highland

5 MILES (8 KM) NORTH-EAST OF KYLE OF LOCHALSH

Palm trees grow in Plockton, encouraged by the mild Gulf Stream air. Also encouraged are small boat sailors, holidaymakers and retired people, who come to this beautiful haven on Loch Carron, with its tidy cottages commanding marvellous views seawards, or inland to the mountains and forests. At one time the harbour, protected by a promontory running out into the loch like a natural pier, was busy with cargo schooners plying to and from Baltic ports, and with the local fishing boats. Herring was taken by sea down to Glasgow, Greenock and the Clyde, and salt and other necessities of life were brought back. All that changed with the railway's arrival at Kyle of Lochalsh in 1898 and the concentration of traffic there. Along the southern shore of Loch Carron and extending far inland is the National Trust for Scotland's magnificent Balmacara estate. Covering thousands of acres of woodland, glittering streams and quiet, reflective lochans, it was bequeathed to the Trust in 1946. To the east along the loch shore, Strome Ferry was another thriving port in its time. It faces across the narrow neck of the inner loch to the ruins of Strome Castle (also National Trust for Scotland), once a formidable stronghold of the Macdonalds. It fell to a siege by the Mackenzies in 1602, allegedly because the castle's womenfolk carelessly emptied water into the gunpowder magazine, so leaving the stronghold defenceless.

'Dominion over palm and pine': looking over Plockton to Loch Carron

Keeping Sunday Special

The West of Scotland has a strong tradition of observing the Sabbath day, and there were riots in Strome Ferry in the summer of 1873, when two steamers with cargoes of fish arrived at the pier in the very early hours of a Sunday morning. Unloading the cargo began, but a crowd of 50 locals gathered, stormed the pier and stopped the work. A handful of police arrived the next day, but were not equal to the situation. Over the next few days the police strength built up to 160 men and only the intervention of the local Free Church ministers defused a potentially violent situation.

At the harbour of Kyleakin, ruined Castle Moil bares its fangs at the sky

ISLE OF SKYE

Highland

Any bonny boat speeding like a bird on the wing over to Skye is due for spectacular views of tremendous cliff scenery and the towering, ominous bulk of the Cuillin mountains. Skye's name is Norse, meaning 'isle of clouds', and the south-western part of the island has some of the heaviest rainfall on the whole of the British coast. All the same, there is a powerful magic about Skye and the principal visitor attractions can become uncomfortably crowded in summer. Car ferries operate regularly to and from the mainland, and a new bridge from Kyle of Lochalsh was opened in 1995. Skye is the largest island of the Inner Hebrides, covering some 535 square miles (1386 sq km). It is a peculiar shape, rather like a giant lobster with the claws to the north-west, and sea lochs bite deep into it, creating numerous peninsulas. The south-western one, Sleat, is known as 'the garden of Skye' for the luxuriance of its vegetation. At Armadale the Clan Donald Centre traces the romantic

Bird on the Wing

Skye cherishes the memory of the Young Pretender, Prince Charles Edward Stuart, and his escape across the Highlands after defeat at Culloden in 1746. On the tiny island of Benbecula in the Hebrides he encountered Flora Macdonald, a shapely young lady of 24, who took him 'over the sea to Skye' by boat, disguised as an Irish maid named Betty Burke, and clad in a blue and white calico dress and quilted petticoat, with a cap to cover his head and face. They landed in Kilbride Bay, north of Uig, and walked to Portree, Flora amused at the immodest way in which 'Betty Burke' raised her skirts to cross streams. They said goodbye in Portree in the inn (now the Royal Hotel). The Prince spent two nights in a miserable hut on Raasay Island, then returned to Skye at a cave on the eastern shore. Now disguised as a manservant named Lewie Caw, he walked to Elgol, where the Mackenzies feasted him in another cave and sent him on by boat to Mallaig. Although there was a huge reward for his capture, the Prince was never betrayed, and eventually escaped to the Continent where he lived out his life in decaying splendour and poverty, dying in Rome in 1788.

history of the Lords of the Isles, whose predatory war galleys maintained an empire in these western seas. The ruined fortress of Dunscaith crowns a headland where, according to legend, the Amazon queen Sgathach ruled long ago, and where the great Ulster hero Cuchulain came to her to be trained in warfare. To the north-west, the black, jagged and sinister peaks of the Cuillins (pronounced 'Coolins'), rising to 3309 feet (1009m) in Sgurr Alasdair, are among the most dangerous mountains in Britain. Boats from Elgol penetrate to the heart of them through Loch Coruisk, possibly the most dramatic loch in all Scotland. North-west again is Dunvegan Castle, stronghold of the MacLeod chiefs in unbroken succession since the 13th century. At one time the castle could be entered only from the sea, but now a bridge lets visitors in over a ravine. Inside, besides a peculiarly hor-rendous dungeon, is the clan's famous fairy flag, a frail piece of tattered silk shot with gold and with crimson spots, which is unfurled in time of desperate peril. According to tradition, it was given to an early MacLeod chief by his wife, who came of the faery race. Delightful boat trips from here to Loch Dunvegan take visitors to see the seals. On the Trotternish Peninsula are the weird battlements and pinnacles of the Quiraing, one of the strangest rock formations in the country; and Flora Macdonald, heroine of the Young Pretender's escape, lies buried in the peaceful graveyard at Kilmuir. The Prince said farewell to her in Portree, on the island's eastern coast, Skye's capital and only town, which is the main touring centre today.

SHIELDAIG
Highland

9 MILES (15 KM) NORTH OF KISHORN

The harbour at Shieldaig, suspended between blue sky and blue water

Vying with Plockton as one of the most attractive villages in the Highlands, Shieldaig, with its white-harled and slate-roofed cottages, lies close to the head of Loch Shieldaig in some of Scotland's most breath-taking scenery. The building of roads since World War II has made this area much more accessible to visitors, for good or ill. Loch Shieldaig was always known for its herrings, though no longer, and indeed the name was originally Sildvik, which is Norse for 'herring bay'. The loch opens into Loch Torridon, by common consent one of the most magical of all Scotland's beautiful sea lochs. To the south lie the mountains, moors and deer forest of the Applecross Peninsula, and a coast road, opened in 1976 to link the scattered crofting settlements together, commanding views over the Inner Sound to Raasay and Skye. Going the other way, east from Shieldaig, the A896 road along Upper Loch Torridon yields awesome prospects of the red sandstone crags of Beinn Alligin and Liathach, rising above 3000 feet (915m). The National Trust for Scotland owns the superb 16,000-acre (6,500ha) Torridon Forest estate, which formerly belonged to the Earls of Lovelace, with its rare eagles and wildcats, deer and mountain goats. There is a good visitor centre and a deer museum.

GAIRLOCH
Highland

7 MILES (11 KM) NORTH-WEST OF KINLOCHEWE

*A*s late as 1960 Gairloch still made its living from the sea, as the Minch fishing boats landed their catches at the pier. Today it is a holiday resort and a centre for touring the wild and dramatic mountains of Wester Ross. Beside the loch of the same name, the village has a sandy beach and there are sailing and sea angling trips to be enjoyed, while the Heritage Museum has a rich store of information about such matters as illicit whisky stills. Loch Gairloch is geologically interesting because it displays the two principal rock types of the north-western coastline. The northern shore is made of reddish Torridonian sandstone, but the southern shoreline is grey Lewisian gneiss. There are sandy beaches along the northern shore, and a coast road leads up to Melvaig with sea views to Skye and the Outer Hebrides. The A832 leads north-east from Gairloch to Poolewe, for boat trips on Loch Ewe and the fabulous Inverewe Gardens (National Trust for Scotland) on the bank of the loch. To the south-east is the beautiful 12-mile stretch of Loch Maree, with the great peak of the Slioch rising above 3,000ft (915m) on its northern side.

Gairloch lies scattered over its greensward, with the loch and mountains beyond

'The lonely sea and the sky' –
the Sutherland shore at
Scourie

❊
SCOURIE
Highland

5 MILES (8 KM) WEST OF LAXFORD BRIDGE
❊

O n this desolate stretch of the Sutherland coast the village is a welcome base for bird-watchers, walkers and anglers in quest of the trout in the region's numerous lochs. Lying offshore is Handa Island, reached by boat from Scourie or Tarbet, an important nature reserve which is now managed by the Scottish Wildlife Trust. Seabirds nest in their tens of thousands on the towering sandstone cliffs – herring gulls and black-headed gulls, guillemots, razorbills, kittiwakes and shags. There are Arctic and great skuas, too, and barnacle geese are seen here in winter. Bird's eggs, fish and potatoes used to be the diet of the island's hardy seven-family population, who had their own 'queen' – the oldest widow. The potato famine of the 1840s drove them away and Handa has ever since been left to the wheeling gulls. This part of the coast running up to Cape Wrath is made mainly of Lewisian gneiss of astounding antiquity. Rocks at Scourie have been dated at nearly 3,000 million years old. It is a country of deep sea lochs and inlets, sandy bays, scattered small islands and very few roads. Grey seals are a familiar sight offshore and in Loch Lexford, with boat trips from Fanagmore to see them. Further north, Kinlochbervie on Loch Inchard developed as a fishing port after World War II.

JOHN o' GROATS
Highland

2 MILES (3 KM) WEST OF DUNCANSBY HEAD

Everyone knows that John o' Groats is the most northerly point of the British mainland, corresponding to Land's End at the south-western tip, some 870 miles (1,400km) away. Strictly speaking, everyone is wrong, as the real northernmost point is Dunnet Head, whose great cliffs rise imposingly above the Pentland Firth some 2 miles (3km) closer to the North Pole. However, the hotel at John o' Groats – there is not much else there – is where the tourists go and where the races and charity walks start or finish. In 1990, when Peter de Savary became the first person ever to own both Land's End and John o' Groats, there were plans for tourist development of the latter, but these did not materialise. John o' Groats commands a view over to the cliffs of Orkney on a clear day. The place takes its name from a Dutchman named Jan de Groot, who operated a ferry from here to South Ronaldsay in the 1490s; or, in another explanation of the name, it is said that the fare was a groat. A mound by the hotel is supposed to be the site of his house. There are boat trips in summer to view the beetling cliffs and the seabirds at Duncansby Head, at Scotland's north-eastern corner, and to the deserted island of Stroma.

The Turning Point

The Pentland Firth, earlier known as the Pictland Firth, is about 14 miles long and from 6 to 8 miles broad. It is a tumultuous and dangerous piece of water, known for sunken reefs and whirlpools, where opposing currents smack into each other to send gouts of water high into the air. Windows in the lighthouse on Dunnet Head, more than 300 feet (90m) above the sea, have been smashed by stones flung up by the raging waves below. At the western end of the firth, however, Cape Wrath was not named for the fury of the sea. Wrath is a corruption of the Norse word *hvarf*, meaning 'turning point', for this was where the Viking longships turned south to range down Scotland's west coast.

Flying the flag for Scotland: the 1870s John o' Groats Hotel

HOLBORN HEAD

Caithness Sandstone

The sandstone of Holborn Head has been quarried since the early 19th century to provide the famous Caithness flagstones; these have been exported to many parts of Britain, including London, to make paving stones. Locally they are used to make the characteristic flagstone fences; in a treeless landscape they make a cheap and efficient material for field boundaries. Where the sandstone is exposed on cliffs and isolated stacks, its horizontal bedding provides superb nesting ledges for seabirds.

Some of Britain's stormiest waters lie between Caithness and Orkney. The meeting of several tides and currents in these narrow straits north of Holborn Head leads to severe turbulence; add the strong winds which seem to blow permanently, and all the ingredients for rough seas are present. The power of the sea has eroded the rock to form some dramatic cliff scenery: many stacks, gulleys, arches and caves are arranged around the headland. Holborn Head lies about 2 miles (3.2km) north-west of Thurso. The walk is approximately 4½ miles (7.2km) long, and starts from Scrabster Harbour car park. It is mostly easy walking, but some sections are on the edge of sheer cliffs, so take care not to stray off the path, especially in windy weather. There are spectacular views of the wild Caithness coastline and the Orkney Islands.

DIRECTIONS

1 From Scrabster Harbour take the harbour road towards the lighthouse. In winter check the inner harbour for gulls, including glaucous gulls, and divers. Further along the road towards the lighthouse, scan the rocks below for waders like turnstones, and watch for divers and black guillemots in the bay.

2 Just before the lighthouse, take a path to the left, passing through a gate and following the path up the hill. The grassy path then leads along the cliff-top to Holborn Head, crossing two stiles on the way.

Look out for skylarks and pipits in the fields and, in winter, flocks of lapwings and golden plovers. In summer, seabirds will be seen on the cliffs below. Kittiwakes are small, dainty gulls with black-tipped wings and a 'kitt-e wake' call. They nest in small, noisy colonies along the cliffs.

3 At the headland are the remains of an Iron Age fort, built in a strategic position over-looking sheer cliffs on one side and an easily defended narrow neck of land on the other. A wall was built across the neck of land as a further defence. From the headland it is possible to look across the Pentland Firth and see large numbers of seabirds in summer; watch fishing boats in case unusual gull species are following them. Pilot whales, white-sided dolphins and common porpoises are seen out to sea and the appearance of a large number of seabirds, especially gannets, feeding excitedly on a shoal of fish is usually a good pointer to where these small whales may appear at the surface.

Bringing the catch ashore at Scrabster

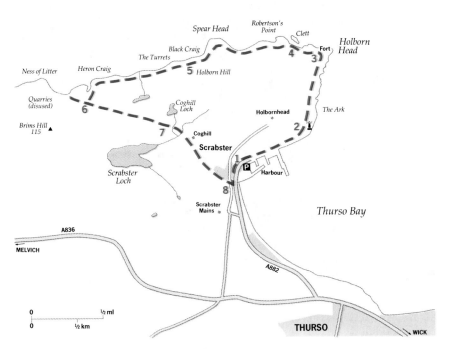

Winter Migrants

In winter a new population of birds appears and, although the nesting ledges may be deserted, the harbour and Thurso Bay will have many divers, sea ducks and gulls over-wintering. Many of these will be from the far north; Iceland gulls, which actually breed in Greenland, large pale-winged glaucous gulls, and the tiny and very rare Ross's gull all turn up from time to time. The sandy beaches and exposed rocks are home to large numbers of waders, especially dunlins, turnstones, sanderlings and redshanks, and rock pipits and snow buntings feed along the high-tide line.

4 Return to the main cliff-top path from the headland, keeping the caves on the right and the wire fence on the left. Beyond the caves, cross the fence for safety as the cliffs here are steep. Continue heading west, with the wire fence on your right.

In summer check the short turf for wild flowers, but be very careful near the edge. The huge rock stack set off from the main cliff is the Clett – a superb nesting habitat for seabirds like fulmars, guillemots and puffins. They are present in summer during the breeding season, but there is so much competition for good nesting ledges that some birds, especially fulmars, visit in the winter to claim to a prime nesting site.

5 Cross the stile in the stone wall and keep straight on towards the quarries; keep to the inland side of the wire fence for safety. Where it is safe to do so, scan the cliffs through binoculars to look for nesting seabirds. Check the rough ground inland on Holborn Hill for short-eared owls and flocks of waders in winter. Look out for the flagstone fences; the pure, damp air of Caithness is ideal for lichens, and many species have colonised these exposed stones.

6 On reaching the gravel road, turn right towards the old quarry; go through the gate and then turn right. This is a good place to look at the Caithness flagstone and see how it was quarried. From the edge of the quarry there is a good view of some sections of the cliff with nesting seabirds. Check the sheltered spots below the cliffs for sea ducks in winter. Take care near the cliff-edge.

7 Return to the gravel road and follow it for about a mile towards Scrabster. On the right is Scrabster Loch and a number of smaller shadow pools, which may hold birds in winter and summer; try not to disturb nesting birds in the breeding season.

8 The gravel road joins a tarmac road which should be followed as far as a postbox. Turn sharp left here, then right down some steps to reach the main road which leads back to the car park at Scrabster Harbour.

❀

BIRDLIFE

Although these rough waters are a hazard to sailors, they are not as damaging to wildlife as might be expected. Ocean currents bring a constant supply of food, and these cold northern waters are a fertile feeding ground for fish, birds and sea mammals. The steep cliffs, with their multitude of nesting ledges, provide ideal conditions for seabirds, and large colonies are found along this coast.

The larger gulls and kittiwakes are present everywhere, following the fishing boats in and out of harbour and loafing in large flocks on half-tide rocks. Guillemots, razorbills and puffins crowd the rock ledges, crevices and grassy cliff-tops in early summer and fly out to the deeper waters of the Firth to feed on sand eels. Fulmars make use of the updraughts on the cliffs to glide and wheel past their nesting ledges, and the occasional great or arctic skua visits from nesting colonies on Hoy. The largest British seabird of all, the gannet, with a 6ft (1.8m) wingspan, is often seen off shore, although none nests on the mainland cliffs.

A Highland rifleman stands lonely watch on the war memorial at Bonar Bridge

BONAR BRIDGE
Highland

14 MILES (23 KM) WEST OF DORNOCH

Rising far away in the mountainous interior of the old county of Sutherland, the River Oykell heads south-east and through the loch called the Kyle of Sutherland to the Dornoch Firth. Where the loch narrows towards the firth, the village of Bonar Bridge grew up. The bridge was built by Thomas Telford to replace the old ferry after a tragic disaster in 1809 which took more than 100 lives. Dornoch Firth resembles an inland loch at this western end, but widens out into a broad estuary nearer the North Sea, with sandy beaches on either shore. The small resort town of Dornoch was Sutherland's county town, and the bishops of Caithness had their cathedral here. It is said that 16 earls of Sutherland lie buried in the church. Inland from Bonar Bridge lies country where the notorious Highland Clearances of the 19th century are not forgotten. The 1st Duke of Sutherland and other landowners removed crofters from the inland valleys to make room for sheep. A road goes to Ardgay and westward through Strath Carron to the church at Croick, where the bewildered local people scratched despairing messages on the glass of the window.

PORTSOY
Aberdeenshire

6 MILES (10 KM) WEST OF BANFF

Restored warehouses at Portsoy, once a busy herring port

The coast of the former shire of Banff, with its high cliffs and fishing villages looking out over the Moray Firth to the cold northern seas, has been hopefully christened 'the Banffshire Riviera'. This particular stretch of it was dominated by the Ogilvie family. One of them, Patrick Ogilvie, Lord Boyne, built the harbour at Portsoy at the end of the 17th century for the export of Portsoy marble, the red and green serpentine stone found in the cliffs here. As he contrived to persuade the Scots parliament to put a ban on the import of marble from abroad, business was gratifyingly brisk. The ban only lasted for six years, but a profitable export trade to France developed and there is Portsoy marble in chimneypieces at Versailles. The fifth Earl of Seafield built a second harbour in 1828, which was destroyed by the sea and rebuilt, as the village flourished on abundant catches of herring. Today Portsoy is a small resort of character for sailing enthusiasts and holidaymakers. The old warehouses and harbour buildings have been nicely restored and souvenir items are still made of Portsoy marble. Not far to the east are the ruins of the once formidable Ogilvie stronghold of Boyne Castle.

SOUTH-EAST SUTHERLAND

This part of Sutherland is an area of contrasts, clearly shown on this 69-mile (111km) planned tour. Sandy beaches separate holiday resorts on the coast. Inland there are huge areas of sheep farms and deer forests. Two vastly wealthy men – a duke and an industrialist – cast very different shadows.

➤➤➤➤

DIRECTIONS

Leave Dornoch on the A949 Castle Street, and at the war memorial turn right on to the B9168 (sp. Wick). After a further 2 miles turn right on to the A9. Continue on the A9 and cross the head of Loch Fleet by a causeway, The Mound. Continue into Golspie. Continue on the A9 past Dunrobin Castle and Carn Liath and on along the coast to Brora. Pass the clock tower, then cross the river bridge and turn sharp left, unclassified

(sp. Brora Heritage Centre and Recreation Area). Continue as the road becomes a single track. Pass through Rogart and, at the main road, turn right on to the A839 (sp. Lairg). In Lairg follow the Lochinver signs and turn right across the River Shin to leave by the A839. In ¾ mile branch left on to the B864 (sp. Invershin) and follow a single-track road through Achany Glen and past the Falls of Shin Visitor Centre. Continue on the B864, and in 1¼ miles turn left on to the A837 (sp. Bonar Bridge) and re-cross the River Shin. After ½ mile turn right on to the A836 for Invershin and continue to Bonar Bridge. Here turn left on to the A939 (sp. Dornoch, Wick A9), passing by Spinningdale to reach Clashmore. In ¼ mile turn left at the junction of the A9 and the new approach road from the Dornoch Firth Bridge Road. Continue for 1¼ miles and turn right onto the A949 for the return to Dornoch.

The quiet town of Lairg – the unexpected home of Europe's biggest one-day sheep sales

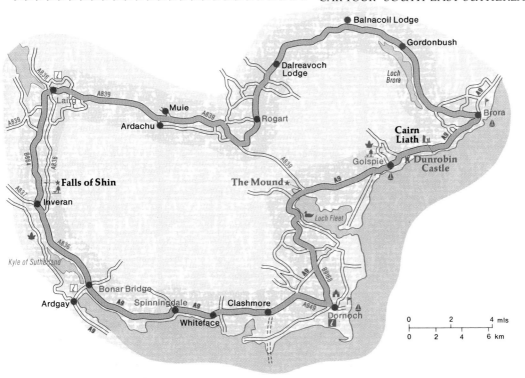

>>ON THE TOUR>>

Dornoch
Golfers come to Dornoch from all over the world. The Royal Dornoch course lies between a long sandy beach and colourful banks of gorse. A footpath overlooks it on the way to Embo. In the attractive square, Dornoch Cathedral was first used for worship in 1239. One group of stained glass windows commemorates Andrew Carnegie, the multi-millionaire philanthropist who retired from business in America to spend most of his time at nearby Skibo Castle. In a garden in the Littletown district, a stone marks the spot where in 1722 poor, demented Janet Horne was the last 'witch' burned in Scotland.

The craft centre in the square at Dornoch is also the entrance to the old town jail. The Old Post Office and Tourist Information Centre has a small exhibition on the area which is open all year.

The Mound
In 1816 Thomas Telford's causeways and bridge over the river Fleet here made the dangerous ferries on the coastal route redundant. Later, The Mound was also used by the Dornoch Light Railway, which branched off the main line to the north.

Golspie
Created from a few fishing huts to house victims of the Sutherland clearances, Golspie is now a comfortable town with a long beach and a golf course, as well as the popular Big Burn Walk. There is also a steep footpath (take care) to the summit of Beinn a'Bhragaidh which is crowned by a monument to the first Duke of Sutherland.

Dunrobin Castle
In mid-Victorian times the second Duke of Sutherland commissioned Sir Charles Barry, architect of the House of Commons, to remodel the ancient family seat. It was originally a square keep, but as it now stands, Dunrobin is almost a palace in the French style, and the grandest house in the north of Scotland. It has many public rooms, a museum and smaller displays including the estate's old steam-powered fire engine. Beautiful formal gardens border the sea.

Brora
A mixture of holiday resort and industrial town, Brora has an exhilarating, breezy beach, a good golf course and excellent salmon fishing, as well as a malt whisky distillery and a woollen mill to visit. There are many interesting Pictish sites to visit in the surrounding area.

Rogart
A scattered crofting village in a maze of roads above the upper valley of the River Fleet, Rogart is a stop on the long Lairg loop of the Inverness-to-Thurso railway. There is a monument to Sir John Macdonald, first prime minister of Canada. His family originated in the area and were among those turned out at the time of the Clearances.

Lairg
This road-junction village and popular angling centre holds the biggest one-day sheep sales in Europe. The countryside here is wild and beautiful, and the Ferrycroft Countryside Centre tells the story from the Ice Age to the present. The dammed waters of Loch Shin power a hydroelectric station. The little hill known as The Ord is a good viewpoint, with an archaeological trail.

Bonar Bridge
Telford built the first bridge over the Kyle of Sutherland here, but the modern structure dates from 1973. Salmon in great numbers swim through the narrows on their way to the spawning grounds, and the Kyle is also a fine sea trout water. Fish passes here allow the salmon free passage upstream; there is a famous salmon leap at the Falls of Shin.

PETERHEAD
Aberdeenshire

27 MILES (44 KM) NORTH OF ABERDEEN

Old Mr Melancholy

It was at Peterhead late in December 1715 that the Old Pretender, otherwise King James III of England and VIII of Scots, landed for the one and only time on Scottish soil. His standard had been raised at Braemar in September and a small army of Highlanders rallied to it, to fight an inconclusive engagement at Sheriffmuir in November. James was of a pessimistic disposition, nicknamed 'Old Mr Melancholy', and he soon decided that the cause was hopeless and returned to his exile in France. The young George Keith, 5th Earl Marischal, and his younger brother James, who had ardently and imprudently joined the rising, had to flee to the Continent, too, later to distinguish themselves in the service of Frederick the Great of Prussia. Years afterwards, the Earl Marischal made his peace with the government and returned to Inverugie.

Fishing boats jostle in Peterhead's spacious harbour.

*I*n 1990 Peterhead was the premier whitefish port in Europe, with £70 million worth of catches landed in the capacious harbour of Peterhead Bay. Overfishing of cod and haddock, however, and the European Community's quotas to protect stocks have made the future uncertain. The town has a second string to its bow as a supply base for the North Sea oil and gas rigs. Built of the local red granite, Peterhead is Scotland's most easterly town. It owed its early development to the Keith family, Earls Marischal, who once owned vast estates in the north-east. Their castle at Inverugie, outside Peterhead, is now a melancholy ruin. The Arbuthnot Museum illuminates the history of the town, which in the 18th century became for a time a smart spa for upper-crust patrons of its warm springs. The harbour proved a more durable asset, however; in the 1880s a prison was built on the bay and the felons were put to work on harbour improvements. In the 19th century Peterhead became a leading whaling port, later turning to herring fishing, but overfishing put paid to the herring harvest and Peterhead fishermen turned instead to whitefish.

LOWER LARGO
Fife

2 MILES (3 KM) NORTH-EAST OF LEVEN

The original of one of fiction's most famous characters was born at Lower Largo in 1676. Alexander Selkirk was a shoemaker's son. In 1695 he was summoned to answer for 'indecent behaviour' in church, but he had already run away to sea. Serving on various expeditions in the Pacific, in 1704 he was marooned on Juan Fernandez Island after quarrelling with his captain. He survived there alone for more than four years until a passing English ship rescued him, and his story of his adventures inspired Daniel Defoe's *Robinson Crusoe*. Selkirk died in 1721, and a statue of him in his goatskins adorns the cottage in which he was born. Lower Largo was once a fishing port on Largo Bay, but the last fishing boat was sold in the 1940s and the village is now a retirement colony and holiday resort, with a sandy beach and golf links. Upper Largo, inland, has the church where Alexander Selkirk's parents are buried. Sir Andrew Wood, who led two Scottish ships to a notable triumph over five English vessels off Dunbar in 1498, is also buried there. He had a canal built from his house to the church and liked to be rowed to services in his eight-oared barge.

Looking for a rescue: the statue of Alexander Selkirk was erected in 1885

KINGHORN
Fife

2 MILES (3 KM) EAST OF BURNTISLAND

A family picnic on the beach at Kinghorn, with the town in the background

Rossend Castle at Burntisland is linked with a tale of Mary, Queen of Scots. French poet Pierre de Châtelard fell extravagantly in love with her and wrote passionate verse in her praise. One night he hid under her bed. Discovered, he was ordered to leave court, but he followed the queen to St Andrews and burst into her bedroom there. He was executed in the market square of St Andrews, crying out just before he died, 'Adieu, the most beautiful and the most cruel princess in the world.'

Along the southern shore of the ancient kingdom of Fife stretches a string of little harbours which once supported ports and fishing fleets, but which cater nowadays to holidaymakers and retired people. Kinghorn has a fine spread of sands along Pettycur Bay and good golfing on the links. It was a royal town in the 13th century, and King Alexander III was riding home from Edinburgh here to his beautiful French queen one stormy March night in 1286, when his horse stumbled and he fell to his death over the cliff. A monument was erected 600 years later on the fateful spot, for the king's broken neck was to open the way for Edward I of England to claim authority over Scotland. Further on to the west, Burntisland once had a whaling fleet and a ferry across the Forth to Granton, which ran until 1939. The remarkable church of St Columba with its octagonal tower was the first to be built in Scotland after the Reformation, in 1592. Going the opposite way, east from Kinghorn, Kirkcaldy is the largest town of this region, at the centre of the Fife coalfield and the local lino industry. The excellent town art gallery has a distinguished collection of work by Scottish artists.

FORTH RAIL BRIDGE

Fife/Lothian

On 4 March 1990 a 53-year-old steam locomotive hauled a special train through the mile-long honeycomb of steel girders and struts across the Forth to mark the centenary of one of the great engineering feats of the Victorian age. The Forth Rail Bridge was designed for the North British Railway by two distinguished engineers, Sir John Fowler and Benjamin Baker, who were also the creators of the Metropolitan Railway in London. It took seven years, 51,000 tons of steel, 7 million rivets and the lives of 57 men to build. The bridge has a surface area of 135 acres (55ha), which a 16-strong team takes 6 years to repaint, starting over again as soon as they have finished.

This tremendous construction has stood up to the burden of traffic better than its younger companion, the suspension road bridge which was opened by the Queen in 1964, with towers 512 feet (156m) high and a central span of 3300 feet (1006m). The two bridges replace the ferry which for centuries crossed the river at this point from Queensferry on the southern bank. It was one of the oldest ferry services on record, going back at least 800 to 900 years and involving steamboats, sailing boats and rowing boats in its time.

'To see the Forth Bridge is rather like meeting a popular actress, but with this difference; it exceeds expectations.'
H V Morton, *In Search of Scotland* (1929)

The cantilevered steel bridge disappears into a bank of cloud on its way across the Forth

INDEX